An Illustrated History of
SOUTHERN WAGONS

Frontispiece: The South Eastern's premier goods depot, Bricklayers Arms, circa 1920. This view is taken looking northwest from Upper Grange Road (later Dunton Road) bridge and shows, on the left, the cattle dock and, in the centre, the goods outward shed of 1901, incorporating an earlier structure of 1850. Just out of view to the right is the locomotive depot. As well as the home-owning company's stock, no less than eight other companies' wagons are visible, namely LBSCR, GWR, MR, LNWR, GNR, GCR, CLC and NBR. *National Railway Museum*

An Illustrated History of
Southern Wagons

by

G. Bixley, A. Blackburn, R. Chorley and M. King

Volume 3 -SECR

Oxford Publishing Co

AUTHORS' NOTES AND ACKNOWLEDGEMENTS

Welcome at long last to Volume 3 of our survey of Southern wagons. This will cover those vehicles inherited from the South Eastern & Chatham Railway's Managing Committee, which for convenience we shall refer to as the SECR. In the early days of the Committee, new wagons were charged out to either the Chatham or the South Eastern section respectively. Later, this does not seem to have been done, but whether the two original companies continued to own a portion of the rolling stock is a subject we have not examined.

We must first apologise for the fact that this volume has taken so long to produce, but this was due to matters largely beyond our control. However, the intervening delay has been put to good use and a considerably greater volume of information is now available, compared to 12 years ago. We are also able to report that work on Volume 4, which will deal with the wagons and containers built by the Southern Railway, is well advanced.

Many enthusiasts have contributed to this volume and we thank them all, but special mention must go to Malcolm Parker for assistance with all matters concerning the LCDR. The official records for the goods wagons of this company are extremely meagre and without his assistance this section of the book would have been poor indeed. By comparison, a great deal of SER and SECR material is available at the Public Record Office in Kew, including several wagon registers compiled around 1919. These include details of those relatively few LCDR wagons still in service at that time. In addition, fellow members of the South Eastern & Chatham Society have rendered much assistance, in particular the late Ian Lyle, whilst the drawings saved at Eastleigh by one of the authors and now in the care of the Historical Model Railway Society have proved invaluable.

Finally, we also wish to thank the present owners of Oxford Publishing Co, for allowing us to complete this long unfinished series of volumes. We trust you will find the completed work interesting and worth the rather long wait.

Title page: A view of Ashford Locomotive Works yard, circa 1905. Amongst the wheel tyres, cylinder blocks and other locomotive parts, some wagons are visible. These include an LCDR dropside, several SER coal wagons, three SER/SECR round-ended opens, a dumb-buffered loco coal and a similar William Cory private-owner wagon. The view appears to have been taken from the roof of the carriage in the foreground. *National Railway Museum*

First published 2000

ISBN 0 86093 493 4

© G. Bixley, A. Blackburn, R. Chorley and M. King 2000

Published by Oxford Publishing Co

an imprint of Ian Allan Publishing Ltd, Terminal House, Shepperton, Surrey TW17 8AS.

Printed by Ian Allan Printing Ltd, Riverdene Business Park, Hersham, Surrey KT12 4RG.

Code: 0002/A3

Contents

Authors' Notes and Acknowledgements 4
Chapter 1. General Introduction to SECR Wagons 7
Chapter 2. Livery, Running and Diagram Numbers 14
Chapter 3. Open Goods and Mineral Wagons 20
Chapter 4. Covered Goods Wagons 70
Chapter 5. Livestock Vehicles 91
Chapter 6. Goods Brake Vans 103
Chapter 7. Bolster and Timber Wagons 121
Chapter 8. Road Vehicle Trucks 128
Chapter 9. Special Wagons 132
Chapter 10. Engineer's Department Wagons 138
Chapter 11. Goods Department Travelling Cranes .156
Appendix 1. Southern Railway Numbering of Ex-SECR Wagon Stock 158
Appendix 2. SECR Wagon Stock Statistics, 1899 and 1913 160

Plate 1 The former LCDR goods station at Longhedge, later known as Stewarts Lane, circa 1920. A small portion of Longhedge Works is just visible to the left, whilst in the background the LBSCR's South London line viaduct crosses the site. In the foreground is all the paraphernalia of a working goods depot, including horse-drawn delivery vehicles and a steam lorry belonging to Fulham-based firm John B. Lee & Sons. A further view of this location, taken at approximately 90° to the above, may be found on page 9. *National Railway Museum*

Plate 2 Another view of Bricklayers Arms, almost certainly taken on the same date as our frontispiece. This is the scene from St James' Road bridge, looking west towards the location of the first picture. Apart from the three Holly Bank private-owner wagons in the right foreground, wagons from the following railway companies may be seen: SECR, LBSCR, LSWR, MR, GN, GE, GW, LNWR, CR, L&Y, CLC, GC and NB — 13 in all. In the right background may be seen the LBSCR's Willow Walk goods depot, with an 'E1' class 0-6-0T shunting. *National Railway Museum*

Chapter 1.
General Introduction to SECR Wagons

The South Eastern & Chatham was a railway of contrasts, not only in the area served, but also in its mechanical engineering. On the first count it served the suburbs of southeast London, the industrial belt of the Thames and Medway and also the prosperous, but chiefly rural, areas of Kent and finally the Channel ports of Folkestone and Dover. On the second count, not only were there two entirely separate companies before 1899, but also there were two separate mechanical eras between 1899 and 1923, firstly under the direction of Harry S. Wainwright and later under R. E. L. Maunsell. In effect, therefore, we are considering no less than four periods in mechanical evolution in the years down to 1923.

There were many differences between the railways of the Southern group, but one thing they all had in common and which set them apart from all the other British railways was that their passenger revenue always exceeded that generated by the carriage of goods or minerals. This is not to say that the goods traffic was unimportant, but it was generally domestic or rural in character as might be expected from an area having very little heavy industry or mineral deposits.

This generalisation is undoubtedly true of the territory served by the London, Chatham & Dover Railway. There were a few exceptions of course, such as the Naval Dockyards of Chatham and Sheerness, but their proportion of the total goods traffic would not have been great, nor even would that generated by the Port of Dover. However, when dealing with the South Eastern Railway system, we meet a concentration of industry along the banks of the Rivers Thames and Medway that puts this company's interest in goods and mineral traffic on a much higher level, and this was reflected in the proportion of wagons owned by the two companies, as the following table (*below*) will amply demonstrate .

Of course, many of the riverside industries were well established before the railway arrived; for them the sailing barge was their traditional form of transport and for some it

remained so until they closed. Several cement and paper works had their own internal railway systems that were never connected to the main line. Other firms were connected, but only used the railway for a portion of their business. Collectively, however, there were over 30 private sidings between Angerstein Wharf and Maidstone West and these provided a wealth of goods and mineral traffic that was not to be found anywhere else on the Southern Railway.

To give an overall picture of the goods traffic handled by the South Eastern & Chatham Railway we cannot do better than quote from the *SECR Guide*, published in 1901 by Cassell & Co.

'Not the least amongst the many undertakings of the South Eastern & Chatham Railway is a rapidly growing goods traffic; not only throughout the county of Kent and such portions of Surrey, Sussex, Hampshire and Berkshire as fall within the limits of their joint system, but practically throughout the Continent. For both the Grande Vitesse and the Petite Vitesse transfer of consignments to and from the chief cities of Great Britain and the Continent via Dover, via Folkestone and via Queenborough are so rapidly increasing alike in their value and their importance as to afford indisputable evidence of the favour with which the Company's routes are regarded by both manufacturers and merchants in all parts of Europe.

'In a general sense, the Company's metals chiefly serve the prosperous agricultural county of Kent and similar districts of its neighbouring counties. Hence a very considerable portion of their tonnage is derived from the carriage of grain. Another factor of financial weight is the transit of the world-famed 'East Kent' and 'West Kent' brands of hop, which come from the Canterbury and Maidstone districts, also from the numerous stations that serve the Kentish Weald.

Wagon Stock as at 31 December 1898

Vehicle Type	LCDR	SER	
Open Goods	1077	2836	
Coal Wagons	200	2642	
Coke Wagons	—	28	
Covered Goods	415	638	
Cattle & Meat Vans	156	247	
Goods Brake Vans (including Ballast)	74	202	
Timber Trucks	78	310	
Road Vehicle Trucks	40	32	
Gunpowder Vans	—	8	
Special Wagons (implement/machinery etc)	1*	5	*Six-wheeled road vehicle truck
Ballast Wagons	40	354	
Totals	2,081	7,302	
Route Mileage	198	427½	
Number of wagons owned per route mile	10.5	17	

Source: The Railway Year Book/SECR Accountants Records

'Leaving the question of hay, forage and roots, each of which is of some local importance, we should notice the vast consignments of cherries annually carried from the orchards of Maidstone, Sittingbourne and Teynham districts; also the tonnage of strawberries, raspberries, gooseberries, plums and other soft fruits, which with vegetables, are regularly transported to the chief markets of the Metropolis, the Midland counties, Lancashire and Yorkshire. In connection with the agricultural and horticultural interests of the territories we should notice the Company's intimate traffic relations with extensive nurseries and seed grounds in the neighbourhoods of Reading, Maidstone, Swanley, Catford, Canterbury and Dover. Numbers of sheep are likewise conveyed from the wide tracts of Romney Marsh and the Isle of Sheppey. An extended reference to the food supplies from Reading and Bermondsey; of the heavy fish traffic from the Kent coast and of the transit of oysters from the famous beds of 'Whitstable natives'. Neither will those interested in the production of fine beer as the national beverage forgive us were we to omit reference to the breweries of Northfleet, Gravesend, Rochester, Wateringbury, Guildford, Reading, Ash, Dover, Canterbury and other towns of East and West Kent.

'But it must not be imagined that the Company's districts are in any degree destitute of those heavier classes of goods traffic which throughout the year make regular demands upon their metals and rolling stock. Beyond the enormous tonnage of paper from the mills at Dartford, Maidstone, St Mary Cray, Sittingbourne and Chatham; a heavy consignment of gunpowder likewise from Dartford, from Chilworth and from Faversham; British timber is dispatched from Dorking, sand of the highest class from Reigate, Fuller's earth from Redhill and sandstone from quarries at Sevenoaks. Lastly, we must deal with probably the largest industry on the Company's systems — namely the huge Portland cement and lime works which are to

be found in the vicinity of Northfleet, Greenhithe, Betchworth, Purley and Queenborough, likewise in connection with Chatham, Strood and numerous stations in the Medway valley or in the Sittingbourne district. Here too, we find vast areas of brickfields, also at Faversham, at Pluckley and at Dunton Green, as well as Southborough, at Frant and at Reading.'

Although written in the form of an advertisement for the company, the above is nevertheless a fascinating insight into the traffic of a railway probably at the height of its prosperity. Perhaps because it deals only with the traffic originating on the system it does not mention coal — the biggest traffic of all. The Kent coalfield had yet to be exploited so there is naturally no mention of this, but there were vast quantities of household and specialised coals that reached the area from elsewhere and these would have been distributed to every station on the system. That from the Midlands came all the way by rail, but the majority of this traffic reached the area by sea to be transhipped at every railway-owned wharf on the system, not to mention several private ones. Indeed, that owned by William Cory at Erith was by far the busiest, dispatching in its time several trains per day.

Much was expected of the Kent coalfield when it was first discovered in the early years of the 20th century and many shafts were sunk, but in the event only four mines ever produced a significant quantity of coal. Unfortunately, these mines were deep and expensive to work, so whilst some specialised uses were found for Kentish coal in general it was not popular nor widely used.

More could be written about the goods trains, services and depots served by the railways in the Southeast, but this is a book devoted to wagons, so we will now turn our attention to the works that built them and the men who were responsible for their designs.

Left:
Plate 3 Typical of the various locations at which sea-borne coal was landed in Kent, this shows Whitstable Harbour, probably in the late 1880s. In the foreground is an early South Eastern covered goods wagon, No 462. Part of a batch of 25 vehicles supplied in 1852 to 'Hensons pattern', it was of 5 tons capacity and had a door on one side, supplemented by a roof hatch. These features were typical of mid-19th century covered goods vehicles, when the multiplicity of wagon turntables ensured that the single-door arrangement was of no inconvenience for loading. The roof hatch would also facilitate crane loading of bulkier items. None of these wagons lasted beyond 1898. Also visible is a diagram 1327 round-ended open wagon, No 2402. This was built by Brown, Marshall in 1864, part of a batch numbered from 2305 to 2404. It failed to become SR stock, but 20 of this vintage did so and were allocated SR Nos between 9784 and 9803.
Douglas West Collection, Whitstable

The Works and the Designers

For convenience we will look at the LCDR first, for development of the Chatham wagon stopped in 1899 whilst that of the SER continued into the SECR period. Early LCDR wagon work was apparently carried out at Faversham and possibly Dover, but our story really starts with the opening of Longhedge Works in Battersea, South London, in 1862. This location was frequently referred to as Battersea Works and

both titles appear on some of the drawings of the works buildings and in SECR records.

William Martley was the Locomotive, Carriage and Wagon Superintendent from 1860 to 1874, so presumably the works were built to his requirements. Joseph Cubitt designed the buildings and several still survive at the time of writing (1999). They are of a very pleasing design and, fortunately, later additions made during William Kirtley's time (1874-98) followed the style of the earlier buildings.

Above:
Plate 4 A view of Longhedge goods depot with the works in the background, taken probably around 1905. The photographer is looking across the area seen in **Plate 1**. A good selection of LCDR, SER and private-owner wagons is visible. Note the high brick wall which entirely surrounded the works area. *J. Tatchell Collection*

It seems that at first the wagons were either repaired in the open or they shared a large shed with the carriage stock. A drawing dated 7 February 1878 for a wagon shop shows a building measuring 293ft 6in by 146ft. It had 11 bays along each side served by a traverser down the centre; this would have provided accommodation for 44 wagons. It is not known if this was built but by 1899 there was a carriage and wagon shop on the same site that measured 331ft by 146ft. This contained 21 roads of which nine were said to be for wagon work. This building was served by a traverser running across the front of the shop. In addition, there was a separate sawmill, blacksmith, timber and general store.

Little is known of Longhedge's early C&W work, but from personal experience we can state that Kirtley's carriages were extremely well built. If his wagons were the same then they must have been some of the best in southern England. Clearly the directors had every confidence in Kirtley, as they allowed him to undertake consultancy work in between his Chatham duties, and in the years 1883-5 he designed the rolling stock for the Hull, Barnsley & West Riding Junction Railway and Dock Co. Many of these vehicles were very similar to

contemporary Chatham designs and some may have been identical.

One of the Managing Committee's earliest decisions was to concentrate all future new work at Ashford and it would seem that the last new wagon was built at Longhedge in June 1900. In the September 1901 edition of the *Railway Magazine* there is a very interesting interview with Harry S. Wainwright, as he liked to be known. He says: 'As far as the Carriage and Wagon Department is concerned, the whole of the general repair and maintenance of the Chatham section is done at Ashford, so that only light running and jobbing repairs are now done at Longhedge.' There seems little doubt of the impression he wanted to leave on the readers of the *Railway Magazine*, but the minutes of the SECR Locomotive, Carriage and Wagon Sub-Committee clearly show that about 12½% of the wagon repair work continued to be done at Longhedge until at least March 1912 when that particular report (and presumably the Committee) was discontinued. In 1930 the Southern opened a C&W repair facility in a building that had started life as a goods tranship shed. This was still in use in BR days but by then it did only special work — conversions and the like.

Ashford Works was older than Longhedge, having opened in 1847. The buildings were of various designs that were forever being extended and altered and they were certainly not to be admired for their external appearance. However, from a description circa 1858 we learn the following: 'The length of the carriage and truck house is 645ft, capable of holding 50 carriages and 80 trucks. The store room is 216ft long by 40ft wide and is a perfect model of neatness — the whole arranged with great precision and even elegance.' R. C. Mansell was in charge at this time. He is best remembered for his 'Patent Safety Wheel'. This design, which featured a wood disc centre, was very successful and was used by railways throughout the country, but more of this to follow.

In 1882 William Wainwright took over control of the carriage and wagon department. An excellent description of the works appeared in *Railway News* for 15 and 22 March 1890 and again we quote: 'In the wagon shop (154ft by 159ft) at the time of our visit, 10-ton coal wagons, with the new flap fasteners and other latest improvements were being built, whilst hands were busily employed in repairs, some 80 wagons being renovated every week. Adjoining this department is the shop where Mansell's wood disc wheels are prepared. Every pair of teak segments are weighed and couples of segments of equal weight are put in that particular wheel, it being very important that the wheel should be evenly balanced. The axles are turned in this shop and the wheel bosses prepared to receive them. The wheels are pressed upon the axles by hydraulic pressure of not less than 60 tons. The smithy (204ft by 55ft) adjoins the wheel making shop and it presents a busy scene with its 23 fires, tyre and spring furnaces, and two 7cwt steam hammers. All the wrought ironwork for the carriages and wagons is made here and at one end bearing springs are made and repaired. The ironwork then goes into the fitting shop to be filed and finished; the brake gives no small amount of work, truss bars, hangers, shafts, etc in large numbers being made here.'

There is no mention of the sawmill in connection with the wagon work so presumably this facility was shared with the carriages, but it was a large shop measuring some 320ft by 100ft and at one time wagon repair work was also carried out within it.

In 1896 Harry Wainwright succeeded his father. Harry had first entered the shops in 1882 as a foreman. At some time in the mid-1880s he worked for the London, Tilbury & Southend Railway and for the Manchester, Sheffield & Lincolnshire Railway before returning to the SER in 1889 as Inspector of Rolling Stock. A year later he became the Ashford C&W Works Manager. In 1898 he was appointed Locomotive, Carriage and Wagon Superintendent to the Managing Committee. He was 34 years old, no doubt pleased with his promotion and, with the benefit of hindsight, near his prime. In the same year a new shop, known as 'The Klondike' was opened to the east of the Hastings line. It measured 316ft by 101ft 6in and contained six roads. It was built as a carriage lifting shop but by 1903 it was being used for wagon repairs.

These were difficult times for the newly amalgamated railway. Both the LCDR and the SER were short of wagons, the latter particularly so, and the railway was hiring, purchasing both new and secondhand, and of course building what it could at Ashford. It is therefore very hard to understand why in these circumstances there was so much haste to cease the construction of wagons at Longhedge. New shops were planned to enable Ashford to deal with this additional work, but a photograph dated May 1901 shows these far from complete and wagons being constructed in the open air. Hardly a propitious beginning.

These new shops were situated to the west of the Hastings line in what was officially known as the West Yard, but was more generally referred to as 'The Kimberley'. They comprised what at the time was described as a carriage repair shed 501ft by 158ft with nine roads and a wagon repair shop 501ft by 105ft 6in with six roads. One of the authors was told by an old

Ashford employee that when these shops were new Wainwright had full-sized drawings of engines made on one wall so that he could experiment with livery details. We do not know if the aforementioned wagon shop was used as such in its early days but in 1912 it was described as a carriage lifting and repair shop, so it seems there was a change of mind and that it had taken over the work formerly intended for 'The Klondike'.

In February 1903 Wainwright was able to report to the Locomotive, Carriage and Wagon Sub-Committee that he had made 'a saving of £3,000 in the last half-year on the renewal account for wagons — owing to the highly efficient state of the wagons' and to add 'I can assure the Committee that I am taking every possible step to ensure rigid economy consistent with efficiency.' Clearly he was doing his best to give the Directors what they wanted — reduced costs. So keen was he to keep down costs that in December 1905 Ashford built a batch of 15 open goods vehicles using recovered ironwork to the extent that these wagons retained single wooden brake blocks. Ashford built large numbers of wagons using recovered wheels, axleboxes and other fittings — indeed such practice was not uncommon into the 1950s — but to build a wagon with wooden brake blocks in 1905 leads us to believe that Wainwright was losing his grip on the situation.

That things were beginning to go wrong there is little doubt. It has been suggested that the combined responsibilities of both the locomotive and carriage/wagon departments were too much for one man and this is almost certainly true. It has also been suggested that he failed to pay as much attention to his duties at this period as he should have done. A letter dated 25 March 1904, Harry S. Wainwright to R. R. Surtees, his Assistant, reads: 'Mr Surtees please supply me with the following information — this is wanted immediately.' He got his information the same day, but not a pleasant way of dealing with a very able and senior member of staff.

It seems that Wainwright managed to satisfy the Directors until around 1910. In that year they pressed for the final closure of Longhedge works and complained strongly about the cost of painting engines. In February 1912 it was decided to appoint one A. D. Jones as Outdoor Locomotive Superintendent with responsibility for engine running. A month later the General Manager was dealing directly with rolling stock contractors. Almost certainly, Wainwright was fully occupied with the transfer of work from Longhedge to Ashford, which was not going well. In October 1913 Jones submitted a damning report on the state of the locomotives. Wainwright's response , if any, was not recorded, but the outcome was that he was asked to retire on the grounds of ill health.

His successor as Chief Mechanical Engineer was Richard Edward Lloyd Maunsell, who came from the Great Southern & Western Railway in Ireland, where he had been Locomotive Superintendent and Works Manager. He found Ashford to be in a mess. There were all kinds of staffing and engineering problems, most of which stemmed from the transfer of work from Longhedge.

Maunsell lost no time in bringing in a new management team, but World War 1 was now under way and some of the engineering requirements had to wait until this was over. Maunsell chose as his Assistant and Works Manager G. H. Pearson, who came from Swindon where he had been the Carriage and Wagon Works Manager. From the same establishment came Lionel Lynes — he was appointed to the post of Chief Carriage and Wagon Draughtsman, having held a similar position at Swindon.

The new team soon transformed Ashford into an organisation capable of keeping the SECR rolling stock at work and the establishment was also able to complete a considerable volume of war work. This included spare parts for locomotives in France, a wide range of munitions and, perhaps most interesting in this context, 120 20-ton covered goods vans for the Railway Operating Division, for use overseas.

As soon as conditions permitted, Maunsell made a start on various improvements and in 1920 'The Klondike' shop was converted into a wagon-building facility. Previous wagon construction seems never to have left the original 1847 'truck' shop, despite all the plans to the contrary.

The Grouping was kind to Ashford, unless you happened to be a carriage man. Maunsell became the Southern's new Chief Mechanical Engineer, whilst both Pearson and Lynes retained their old positions but with greater responsibilities. So far as the works was concerned, things carried on as previously for a few years, but it was not long before all the carriage work was transferred away; new construction went to Eastleigh, repairs to Lancing. In return, Ashford gained all of Lancing's wagon repair work, together with almost all subsequent new wagon construction. New underframes were built in what had been the original wagon ('truck') shop, new bodywork was carried out in 'The Klondike', whilst all repair work was concentrated in the two large shops in 'The Kimberley'.

And so we come to the wagons themselves. One of the most noticeable features of SER and LCDR wagons was the similarity that existed between the two companies' designs. A possible explanation may be that some member of the design staff left Ashford to join the Chatham, perhaps to further his career, but the true reason may be more prosaic. Both railways had very similar traffic and both found the same answer. In general, comparison of the two companies' designs finds the Chatham wagon to be the larger and the more heavily constructed. To take an example, both covered goods wagon designs show remarkably similar features and, at the time of writing, there exists in Chatham Dockyard a preserved van which at first sight could pass for either. Very possibly this van was designed by one or other of the two companies — possibly Kirtley doing a spot of consultancy.

As mentioned in our introductory note, comparatively little is known about the Chatham wagons. Very few reached the Southern Railway, in total around 200 vehicles, and even fewer were photographed. The information that has survived tells us that there were a small number of highly standardised designs, at least in the latter part of the 19th century, but the situation may have been very different in the earlier years. If

the variety of LCDR locomotives from the early period is indicative, then almost certainly the same may be said of the early wagon stock. The company standardised its journal centre spacing at 6ft 5in, a dimension at variance with most other railways, and this feature almost certainly contributed to the early demise of the stock. In contrast, early SER vehicles had 6ft 4in spacing, but by the 1870s a dimension of 6ft 8in was adopted and this remained unaltered until the employment of RCH (Railway Clearing House) standards during Maunsell's time.

Rather more is known about SER wagons and it must be said that with their wooden-centred Mansell wheels they certainly looked very different to the wagons of most other British railway companies. We have already noted that the Mansell wheel was a very successful design, but it was expensive to produce and on other railways its use was normally confined to passenger stock. Why then did the SER and SECR use it under wagons? One cannot be certain, but the clue is probably provided in the correct name — 'The Mansell Patent Safety Wheel'. This was developed at a time when casting techniques were not fully understood and it was not unknown for iron wheels to fail in traffic. The Mansell wheel was sound, so why risk using something else? Besides which, the SER did not have to pay the patent fee. The SECR continued to use them for the simple reason that wagon wheels did not incur a very high mileage and could therefore be reused when the rest of the wagon was worn out.

Below:
Plate 5 These vans are a World War 1 design for the War Department. A total of 120 were constructed at Ashford to this design. In fact, these particular examples were built by the LBSCR at Lancing Works but were identical to those completed at Ashford. The SECR also provided 1,070 of its own wagons for the War Department in 1917-18. These included 900 12-ton coal wagons and 120 ballast wagons. Most were sent from Chatham or from Richborough Port. The majority were returned in 1919-21, many being stored in the Canterbury area prior to being made fit to return to traffic. *LBSCR Official*

The other very distinctive feature was the high round ends on the open wagons. Here the LCDR also came to the same conclusion, although the end shape was slightly different. We cannot do better than quote Harry Wainwright in his 1901 interview with the *Railway Magazine*. 'The bulk of our wagon stock are goods wagons of the type known as 'high-ended', which are found to be generally most useful for the class of traffic on this railway.' One only has to look at the photographs of SER wagons loaded with hay or sacks of hops to see exactly what he meant. The SECR owned rather less than the national average number of covered goods wagons, but there was little point in building expensive covered vans when a more versatile sheeted open would suffice. To quote Wainwright again: 'For the purposes of utilising our coal wagons for goods traffic, we have a large number of coal wagons fitted with tarpaulin supports, so that they may be used for carrying goods and the loads sheeted over.'

To gain a deeper insight into SER (and subsequent SECR) policy we have to refer again to the 1890 article in *Railway News*: 'Mr Wainwright (senior) some little time back decided upon designs which, with minor modifications suggested by experience, may be taken as the type of work for many years to come.' How prophetic that statement was to prove, for Harry Wainwright was still building what were basically his father's designs nearly 20 years later. The SER and SECR did experiment with various types of wagon brakes. A very large proportion of the wagons built during Harry Wainwright's superintendency were equipped with either J. Stone's or E. J. Hill's patent either-side brakes. J. Stone was the founder of the well-known railway engineering company of that name, with works alongside the railway at Deptford, whilst E. J. Hill

was a consulting engineer with offices in Victoria Street. Vincent Hill was General Manager to the SECR from 1901 until 1910 and is believed to have been a close relative. The SECR was the only railway company to use Stone's brake, but Hill's brake gear was also employed to some extent by the Midland Railway and also by the Barry Railway in South Wales.

Quite a number of wagons were purchased secondhand during Harry Wainwright's time. Some of these were ex-contractors' ballast wagons. It was not unusual for a railway company to buy these upon completion of a contract, for further engineering department use. However, in the case of those acquired from Price & Reeves in 1901 (diagram 1352) this deal may have been arranged beforehand, as they were virtually normal railway wagons; indeed the SECR classed them as open goods wagons. They were certainly a cut above the usual contractors' vehicles. Then there were several purchases of ex-private-owner coal wagons. In these instances the SECR may have been pursuing a policy of ridding its own area of PO wagons in the same way as the Midland Railway tried to do. Whilst this policy is not recorded as such, the best evidence of it is the large number of 12-ton RCH minerals (diagrams 1357/58) purchased new in some sort of agreement with coal factors William Cory. Wagons were also hired from time to time, such was the perennial shortage of stock. There was a duplicate list of wagon numbers, commenced in September 1912. These used the prefix letters 'A', 'B' and 'C'. The 'A' wagons were former private-owners, the 'C' wagons were Midland Railway vehicles on loan, whilst it is believed the 'B' series were Hull & Barnsley stock, also on loan.

Maunsell was not satisfied with the wagon fleet as he found it in 1913. As a stopgap he built two small batches of timber-

framed open wagons, unusual for not being equipped with crib-rails. He also continued the 'reconstruction' of some older wagons — in particular the better examples of LCDR stock — but for the future he instructed Lynes to design a standard steel underframe, 17ft long. The design used RCH wheels, but differed from the RCH underframe in that the independent drawbars pulled on the middle cross-members, rather than being continuous, and also self-contained buffers were provided. This design was used for five and seven-plank opens, a two-plank ballast, twin bolsters, a road vehicle truck and a covered goods van. The details were all reminiscent of Great Western practice, as might be expected given their designer's origins. Prototype vehicles of each type were constructed, referred to as 'pattern wagons', before general production commenced. In this way any design faults could be eliminated before too many vehicles were in traffic. The covered van and brake van designs used a feature unique to British wagons, namely the high semi-elliptical roof profile normally associated with passenger stock.Whilst satisfactory on the heavily-constructed brake van, it was destined to give endless trouble on the covered goods vehicle. Despite this, the design feature was perpetuated on over 9,000 similar Southern Railway vehicles, but more of this in Volume 4.

Finally, we include a table giving the breakdown of the number of SECR wagons taken into Southern Railway capital stock at the Grouping, which will be worthy of careful study by modellers wishing to portray a typical SECR goods yard scene. These are based on the SR renumbering registers and not on the totals shown on the diagrams — there is some variance between the two sets of figures and so should not be relied upon to the last digit. Figures quoted by the company were not unknown to vary slightly depending on their source.

SECR Wagons Taken into SR Stock after 1 January 1923 (Including Outstanding Orders)

Vehicle Type	Capacity in Tons												Totals	% of Total
	6	7	8	9	10	12	13	15	20	25	30	35		
Open goods	4	7	388	14	4,772	2,121	—	—	—	—	—	—	7,306	60¼
Mineral	—	—	—	—	70	1,851+	—	59	—	—	—	—	1,980	16½
Covered goods	92	—	639	—	550	—	—	—	—	—	—	—	1,281 ⎫	11
Fruit & meat vans	6	—	18	—	8	—	—	—	—	—	—	—	32 ⎭	
Cattle wagons	13	—	45	1	241	—	—	—	—	—	—	—	300 ⎫	2¾
Special cattle wagons	—	20#	7#	12#	—	—	—	—	—	—	—	—	39 ⎭	
Goods brake vans	4	—	—	1	172*	4	2*	—	90	40	—	—	313	2½
Timber/bolster wagons	2	—	124*	—	64*	102*	—	—	—	—	—	—	292	2¼
Road vehicle trucks	—	—	1	—	51	2	—	—	—	—	—	—	54	½
Machinery/well wagons	—	—	—	—	—	—	—	2	19	—	—	—	21 ⎫	
Shunting trucks	9	—	—	3	—	—	—	—	—	—	—	—	12	
Gunpowder vans	—	23	—	—	—	—	—	—	—	—	—	—	23 ⎬	½
Aeroplane trucks	10	—	—	—	—	—	—	—	—	—	—	—	10 ⎭	
ED ballast wagons	25	1	77	—	180	120	—	—	14	—	—	—	417 ⎫	
ED ballast brake vans	—	—	—	—	22	—	—	—	1	—	—	—	23 ⎬	3¾
ED rail/sleeper wagons	—	—	—	—	—	4	—	—	—	—	12	6	22 ⎭	
Totals	165	51	1,299	31	6,130	4,204	2	61	124	40	12	6	12,125	100

Notes

1. Figures marked * include wagons permanently coupled in pairs.
2. Figure marked + includes 200 wagons allocated to locomotive coal traffic.
3. Figures marked # show capacities as per SR diagrams. Those actually painted on the vehicles varied by up to 2 tons.
4. The totals in the table do not agree with the 1923 Company returns, partly because ED (engineering department) stock (non-revenue-earning) was excluded from such returns. Also several hundred wagons were withdrawn from stock in the early months of 1923 before the renumbering scheme was worked out.
5. Some wagons were withdrawn before receiving their allocated SR numbers.
6. The Southern Railway reclassified almost 2,000 wagons as open goods vehicles where previously they were considered as coal (ie mineral) wagons. These are shown above as open goods wagons, as per the SR register.
7. The 39 special cattle wagons, 10 aeroplane trucks and 12 fruit vans were reclassified as passenger stock after 1923.
8. The Southern Railway ordered 1,128 more wagons to SECR designs subsequent to the Grouping. Details of these are as follows:
   150 10-ton five-plank open goods wagons (SR diagram 1347) — SR order A15;
   500 12-ton seven-plank open goods wagons (SR diagram 1355) — SR order A28;
   100 12-ton covered goods wagons (SR diagram 1426) — SR order A26;
   300 10-ton cattle wagons (SR diagram 1515) — SR orders A25, A106 and A165;
   20 25-ton goods brake vans (SR diagram 1560) — SR order L110;
   35 20-ton machinery wagons (SR diagram 1681) — SR orders E109 and A1096;
   3 20-ton ballast brake vans (SR diagram 1748) — built by C. Roberts Ltd.

In addition, order A29 for 20 25-ton goods brake vans was cancelled in favour of purchasing a similar number of ex-War Department LSWR diagram 1549 vehicles from Messrs Cohen Armstrong's Disposal Board in 1924. These were purchased under order E44.

Left:
Plate 6 A typical Chatham section goods train. Ex-LCDR 'B1' class 0-6-0 No 613 stands at Herne Bay in August 1905. Apart from the fourth wagon in the train — LSWR stone wagon (later SR diagram 1308) — all other vehicles are of SER or LCDR origin. This would be the norm until the introduction of common user policies during World War 1. *L&GRP*

Chapter 2.
Livery, Running and Diagram Numbers

As was discussed in Volume 1, there is probably more controversy over the subject of liveries than any other aspect of rolling stock history. The simple truth of the matter is that we do not know the exact shades of colour used some 80 or more years ago. In those days paints were hand mixed and no matter how carefully this was done there must have always been some variation. Lettering is another problem, but here at least photographs may be of assistance. In the majority of cases, the lettering layouts shown on the drawings are taken from actual examples.

The London, Chatham & Dover Railway

The basic overall colour was grey, with black running gear and white lettering. The actual shade of grey is, however, the subject of some debate. In 1896 *Moore's Monthly Magazine* recorded the colour as dark grey, whilst an 1890 photograph gives a comparison that the colour was darker than that being used by the Midland Railway. The *Railway Magazine* in 1904 made the comparison that LCDR wagons had been grey,

whereas the SECR colour was dark grey, suggesting a lighter colour was in use before 1900. **Plate 7** suggests a fairly light colour, but this is not confirmed by some other photographs. It is therefore concluded that a medium grey was the 'correct' colour, even if this varied somewhat in practice. Body ironwork was sometimes 'blacked-up', to use the contemporary term, but this was by no means universal in its application. There is no evidence of this in **Plate 7**.

Lettering was in approximately 6in-high characters, the company initials appearing in the form LCDR, usually high up, well spaced out and either side of the centre doors (if fitted). The number appeared near the right-hand end, at low level, whilst the load was usually in italic script near the lower left-hand end, in the form 'To Carry 10-0-0' or similar. The tare weight appeared below the wagon number, in either small italics or block figures. On bolster wagons and other vehicles with a low side rail, the company lettering was much more closely spaced, allowing the number, carrying capacity and tare to be placed on either side of the company initials, in the usual positions. **Figures 58, 59** and **64-6** will make this clear.

Left:
Plate 7 Photographs of wagons in LCDR livery are extremely elusive. Most tend to be fortunate background enlargements of locomotives or other views and this is no exception. Open wagon No 2370 (built by Metropolitan in 1881, later SECR No 11361) and covered goods wagon No 14XX (part of a batch built by S. J. Claye in 1876) are seen at Longhedge, freshly outshopped in what appears to be a light or medium grey colour. The visible lettering layouts have been used to illustrate **Figures 8** and **34**. *M. Parker Collection*

The only exception to the grey livery for LCDR wagons appears to be those few with Westinghouse brakes or pipes, where the Company Appendix to the *Book of Rules and Regulations to the Working Timetable* dated March 1898, states these were painted in the passenger stock colour, but is no more specific than this. We therefore presume the colour to be brown (the carriages were varnished teak), with perhaps yellow or more probably white lettering in the same format as on the goods-rated vehicles. There is no mention of white for roofs, so presumably these were grey. Wagon tarpaulins appear to be black and were lettered as shown in **Figure 1**. On 25 July 1899 there were 2,292 in service, all maintained by a contractor named Briggs. One is visible in **Plate 170**. Wagon

numberplates do not appear to have been provided by the LCDR.

The South Eastern Railway

The ordinary wagons were painted red with black running gear and white lettering. In 1881 the body colour was described as Venetian red, by 1896 the official description was red oxide, whilst in the same year *Moore's Monthly Magazine* described the colour as light red. By 1904 the *Railway Magazine*, somewhat unhelpfully, used the term brick red. The body colour was normally used for solebars, headstocks and buffer guides as well.

The Mansell wheels were very smart, at least when new. The tyres and wheel centres were white, the timber segments were treated with Copal varnish and to finish the job off the axles were blue. Open-spoke wheels were black, but again the axles were blue. Roofs were finished in white lead paint. Blacked-up body ironwork was perhaps more common on SER wagons than on the LCDR or the SECR.

The brake vans were painted differently from the other goods stock — at least those described as being for passenger or goods trains (SR diagram 1552) were so treated. The 1886 specification quotes: 'body lake, fine lined vermilion. Underframe black, fine lined vermilion'. Note there is no mention of red ends. *Moore's*, in 1896, states: 'break [sic] vans had dark red-brown sides, bright red ends and black ironwork'.

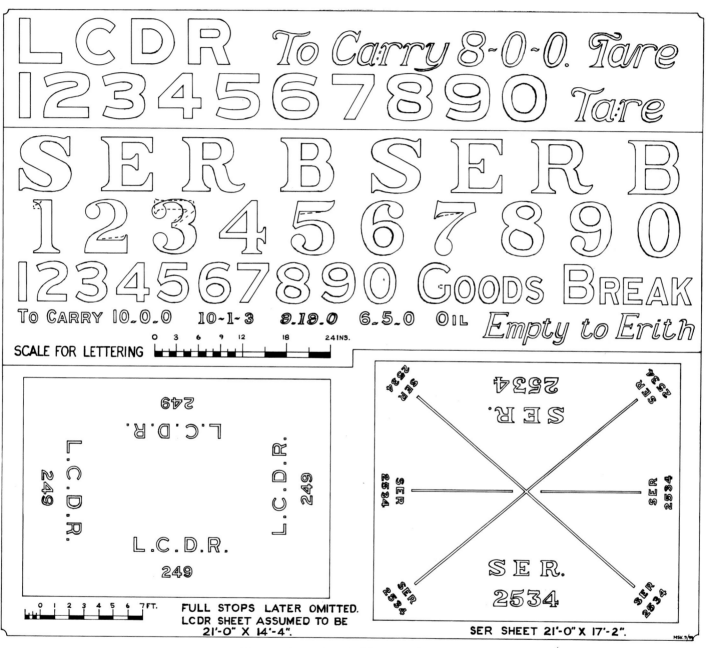

Figure 1. Examples of LCDR and SCR lettering

Before leaving the subject of body colour it is worth noting that the *Locomotive Magazine* reported in 1898 that 'some smart looking new covered box wagons have just been delivered to the SER by the builders, the Ashbury Carriage & Iron Company, painted dark red with white lettering'. These would have been SER Nos 8950-9049 and it is possible that the colour referred to was the passenger stock lake livery.

All lettering was white, serifed and unshaded on ordinary wagons, but the brake vans, as already mentioned, often proved the exception to these rules. The company initials 'SER' appeared at the left-hand end usually low down on the bottom plank or side rail, but high up on cattle wagons and goods break vans. The number usually appeared on the right-hand side in a corresponding position. Both company initials and wagon numbers were in approximately 7in-high characters, unless the construction of the wagon prevented this, for example on timber trucks where they were 3¼in high. The carrying capacity appeared in the form 'To Carry 8-0-0', usually on the side rail or solebar in small block letters, below the company initials. The 'T' and 'C' were 1¾ in high, the other letters were 1½ in high. The tare weight appeared in a similar position, but directly below the wagon number. Finally the running number appeared again on the wagon end, usually in

2½in or 5¼in numerals, either centrally above the draw hook or to the right of it, towards the top of the headstock. Alternatively, the number might appear centrally on the bottom plank or, on fitted vehicles, above the brake hose. These numerals were often in block characters, instead of the serifed style employed on the wagon sides. Naturally there were some exceptions to these rules, dictated by the construction of the wagon and some of these may be seen in the drawings. **Figure 1** gives details of SER lettering.

Wagon tarpaulins were 21ft by 17ft 2in, black with a double red cross, used to assist in centering the sheet on the wagon, with white lettering. At 25 July 1899 there were 8,062 in use, all maintained at Ashford Works. Again **Figure 1** gives details. As with the LCDR, wagon numberplates were not provided, however, a few wagons carried a works plate, recording the date and place of construction.

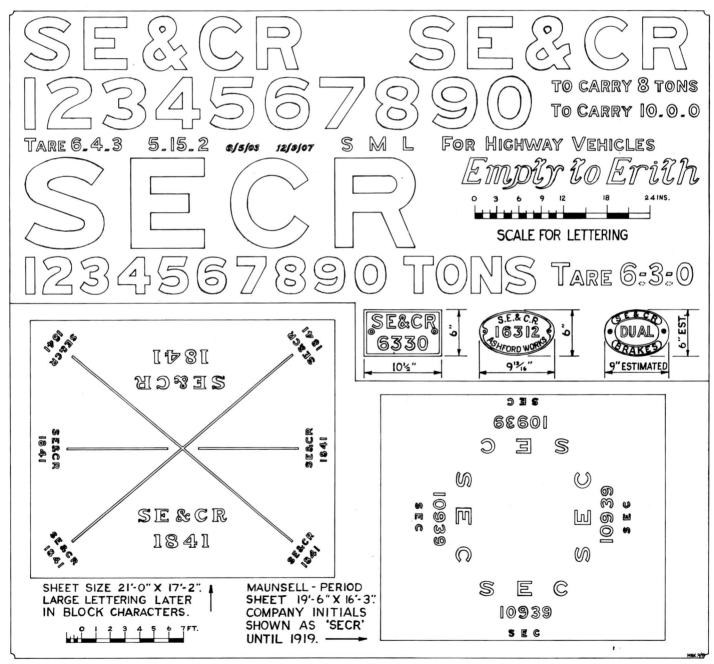

Figure 2. Examples of SECR lettering

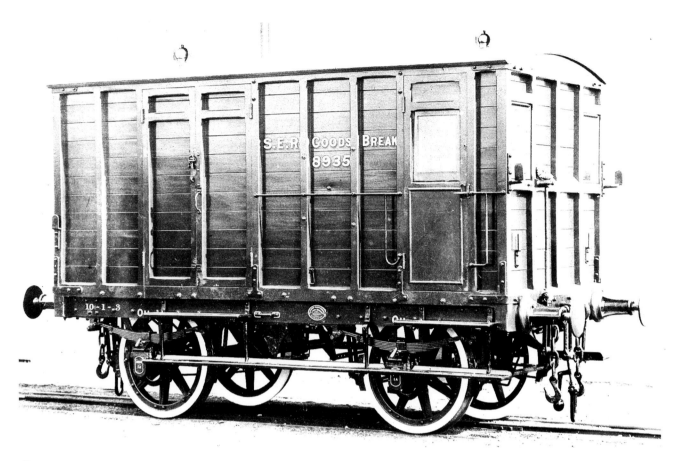

Above:
Plate 8 Diagram 1553 goods break van No 8935, one of 20 completed by Gloucester Railway Carriage & Wagon Co in 1898. This clearly shows the dark red-brown sides, bright red ends and blacked-up body ironwork. The buffer guides are also black. Note that the lettering is in a block style, shaded in black. These features were usually confined only to break vans. *GRCW Co*

The South Eastern & Chatham Railway

The only major change was in the basic body colour, from red to grey, of a darker shade than that formerly used by the LCDR. Officially, this was described as lead colour and normally included solebars, headstocks and buffer guides. A 1900 specification for a goods brake van calls for lead grey inside and out, with a white lead roof. There is no mention of bright red ends; a matter further discussed in Chapter 6. At this time wagon axles were still blue, but all else below solebar level was black.

Lettering continued to follow the SER layout, but with block 7in characters in place of the serifed style previously used. The lettering had a somewhat 'hand executed' style, rather than appearing stencilled. At first the company initials SE&CDR or SECDR were used, but these were soon abbreviated to SE&CR. End numerals were now almost always in the centre of the lowest plank, in either 5¼in, 3¼in or 2⅛in characters. Where the design of the wagon dictated, smaller lettering was used, for example on bolster wagons, machinery trucks and road vehicles trucks — 3in-high lettering being the usual size. Goods brake vans, again, had styles peculiar to these vehicles. Several SECR lettering diagrams survive in the Historical Model Railway Society collection and it is probable that such a diagram was

prepared for every type of wagon. Where known, the details shown on the drawings follow these examples, or are taken from photographic evidence.

Cast rectangular wagon plates were provided on new stock from about 1910 onwards, painted black with the lettering picked out in white. Dual-fitted wagons also had an oval plate on the solebar, lettered 'SE&CR DUAL BRAKES'. This had white lettering, but the background may have been blue or red. An example may be seen in **Plate 109**. Tarpaulin sheets varied little from SER practice, merely having a revised company title; however, by 1920 the company title had been abbreviated to 'SEC' only. By then the size had been altered to 19ft 6in by 16ft 3in

After Maunsell took over, the style of lettering changed considerably and possibly the shade of grey was made darker, more akin to the GWR. These processes may not have started until c1917. Company initials ('SECR') now appeared in 12in letters across the wagon, wherever possible. For bolster wagons and the like, 6in letters became standard. The number appeared on the left-hand bottom plank in 5in numerals, the carrying capacity on the right-hand side, also in 5in high characters. Tare weights normally appeared on the solebar — the letter 'T' and numerals being 3in high, the other letters being 2in high. Finally the wagon number was now omitted from the ends, but there were occasional exceptions to this.

Above:
Plate 9 Standard Maunsell period lettering is carried by diagram 1347 open goods wagon No 9821, completed by Cravens of Sheffield in 1920. It later became SR No 14149. Notice how dark the base colour now appears. Some vehicles had the grey livery applied overall, even including the brakes and running gear — very much the practice at Swindon, from whence came both G. H. Pearson and L. Lynes the Assistant Chief Mechanical Engineer and Ashford Works Manager and Chief C&W Draughtsman respectively. *SECR Official*

There seems to have been one exception to the general use of grey after World War 1, concerning fitted wagons of both open and covered goods types. A personal recollection of the period states that these wagons were painted dark brown, as were many of the passenger coaches and the passenger-rated vans such as horseboxes. This policy also had a following at Swindon, so it may well be accurate. A sample panel of this brown survives on the Bluebell Railway and this shows the colour to be a very dark brown, without any hint of red, much darker than GWR chocolate.

Maunsell continued to provide numberplates, but these were now oval in shape. Examples of SECR lettering, numberplates and tarpaulin sheet's appear in **Figure 2**.

Diagrams and Numbering

The LCDR produced a drawing entitled 'Diagrams of Wagon Stock', showing small-scale sketches of the vehicles, with leading dimensions. Each individual drawing does not appear to have been allocated a diagram number, so its use for identification purposes is limited. This drawing would have been periodically updated as necessary.

LCDR wagon numbering was well organised, at least from about 1870 onwards. Each type of wagon was allocated a block (or several blocks) of numbers, according to the table below. In 1899 these were renumbered into the SECR series, following on from the then highest allocated SER numbers, in the same order as their LCDR numbers. We are indebted to Hugh Hughes, who researched and compiled the following table.

LCDR Goods Wagon Numbering

Wagon Type	LCDR Nos	SECR Nos	Total
Coal wagons (dropside)	1-200	11392-591	200
Brake vans and ballast brake vans	201-50, 2201-24	11866-939	74
Timber and bolster wagons	251-300, 2101-28	11592-669	78
Highway vehicle trucks	301-41	11940-80	41
Open goods wagons	400-79, 500-697, 700-999, 1101-250, 1681-879, 2251-400	10315-1391	1,077
Cattle wagons and meat vans	1000-70, 2000-84	11670-825	156
Covered goods wagons	1251-666*	9900-10314	415
Ballast wagons	6001-40	11826-65	40
		Total	2,081

*One number vacant between 1300 and 1306.

The SER produced numbered diagrams for its wagon stock, with the prefix 'AS' — perhaps signifying 'Ashford Stock' or 'Ashford Sketch'. One wonders if this was a SECR addition; if so, were LCDR diagrams prefixed 'LS' — 'Longhedge Stock'?

In the case of wagon numbering, the series commenced at 1 and reached 9899 by mid-1899, although vehicles numbered above 9049 were ordered in the name of the SECR and probably appeared with the new company initials. At first there was a definite attempt to keep certain blocks of numbers for certain types of stock, but as reuse of vacant numbers began, this proved difficult to keep up. When numbers were being used for the first time then complete blocks were allocated. As the original wagons wore out they would be replaced, sometimes piecemeal. It would then be possible to find new blocks of numbers, broken by odd survivors from an earlier period. Generally, wagons built on the renewal account took reused numbers, those on capital account took new numbers at the upper end of the list. This was not a universal rule, since if enough blanks existed lower down the list then these could be reused for new wagons charged to capital account as well.

The SECR allocated diagrams to most of its wagon stock. Those which failed to get a separate diagram were mostly odd conversions, secondhand purchases and the like. All diagrams were prefixed 'S' — perhaps for 'sketch', as if to underline the fact that they were not full drawings in the manner of a general arrangement or detailed working drawing. The sequence of numbering is fragmented, so perhaps the same number series was also used for the general arrangement drawings which did not have a prefix. The quality of the diagrams varied. Some were very accurate, others very poor. In most instances they were correct for some but not all wagons allocated to that diagram. Most LCDR vehicles had new diagrams prepared and several of these are suspect. For example, both 15ft and 16ft covered goods wagons appeared on the same diagram, whilst two different bolster wagons used the same sketch, with dimensions altered to suit. Maunsell period diagrams are, as one might expect, rather better than average — probably mirroring GWR practice at Swindon.

SECR wagon numbering followed SER practice, all SER wagons keeping their old numbers. New numbers above the LCDR block (9900-11980) were used from 1900 onwards. The highest number used was 16430, in 1922, but many other numbers further down the list were reused, including some allocated to former LCDR vehicles. There were also three duplicate number series, prefixed 'A', 'B' and 'C', used for secondhand purchases and wagons on hire or loan.

The Southern Railway

The Southern Railway produced its own series of diagrams, generally perpetuating the errors inherent in the SECR diagrams, but in some instances separated out wagons where their dimensions varied, even fractionally. There was no consistency to the practice, as some obvious errors remained uncorrected. The diagram numbers are summarised in the table **below**.

The company also renumbered the entire wagon stock after the Grouping, sorting the wagons by origin, type and in ascending order of capacity in the form shown in the table **right**. Not surprisingly, this procedure took several years to complete and wagons in pre-Grouping livery were not uncommon until the early 1930s. The initial SR renumbering scheme was very logical, but soon became obscured by changes, additions and the reuse of numbers for new stock. Fuller details of SR numbering may be found in Appendix 1 on pages 158-9, together with the diagram numbers, which were arranged along similar lines. Examples of pre-Grouping numbering will be given in the relevant chapters.

Summary of Southern Railway Diagram and Wagon Running Numbers

Type of Vehicle	SR Diagram Nos	Diagram Nos of Ex-SECR Stock	SR Running Nos	Running Nos of Ex-SECR Stock
Open goods and mineral wagons	1301-400	1324-60	1-42000	9639-18727, 19079-228, 28501-9000
Covered goods wagons	1401-60	1419-27	42001-50000	44627-5907, 47101-200
Refrigerator, banana and insulated vans	1461-80	None	50001-1000	None
Ventilated meat vans	1481-500	1489-91	51001-500	51221-40
Cattle wagons	1501-40	1512-8	51501-4500	52519-881, 53391-627
Goods brake vans	1541-90	1552-60	54501-7000	55183-515
Bolster, timber and batten wagons	1591-640	1601-10	57001-60000	57931-8222
Road vehicle trucks	1641-70	1654-7	60001-1000	60318-71
Special vehicles (glass, aero, well, machinery)	1671-700	1679-81	61001-200	61039-59, 61086-98, 61151-72
Gunpowder vans	1701-10	1703	61201-300	61223-45
Miscellaneous wagons	1711-30	None	61301-500	None originally, 61341-8 later
Ballast wagons, ballast brakes and plough vans	1731-80	1741-8 and 1761 (later)	61501-3500	62084-527, 62030-2
Locomotive and marine coal wagons	In open goods range	In open goods range	63501-4500	63751-4040, 64352-92
Rail and sleeper wagons	1781-849	1794-6	64501-800	64604-21
Service and departmental stock (mostly SR conversions)	1850-2000	Few diagrams allocated	1s-1999s 01s-01290s	Various

Notes
1. Duplicate stock not generally included. A few were later added to the list.
2. Vehicles built to SECR designs between 1923 and 1942 are included.
3. SR diagram numbers from 1-1300 and from 2000 onwards were allocated to passenger stock.

Chapter 3.

Open Goods and Mineral Wagons

These two classes of wagon, not surprisingly, form by far the largest proportion of the stock — in total well over 9,000 vehicles at the Grouping, comprising almost 77% of the entire wagon fleet. If judged on numbers alone, then this chapter should occupy three-quarters of the book; as it stands, however, we have allocated almost one-third of the volume to the subject.

The distinction between open goods and mineral wagons varied over the years and the Southern Railway reclassified many vehicles previously described by both pre-Grouping companies as coal (ie mineral) wagons into the open goods wagon category in 1923. The distinction between the two classes was strictly observed in earlier years, at least on paper if not always out on the line, but by the formation of the SECR the distinction was becoming blurred, only to re-emerge some 10 years later with the appearance of the many Railway Clearing House (RCH) specification mineral wagons. These were true mineral wagons, whereas most of the earlier coal wagons could be mistaken for open goods vehicles and, indeed, were often used as such. By 1915 the earlier coal wagons were probably judged too small for coal haulage and it is generally these that the Southern Railway reclassified as open goods vehicles. This probably reflected their use by 1923 and is also shown in the table of statistics reproduced on page 13. However, the tables reproduced in Appendix 2 reflect the pre-Grouping classification.

For the purpose of study, we intend to consider this large subject in four groups, divided partly by origin and partly by date of construction. These are:

1. Vehicles of London, Chatham & Dover Railway origin.
2. Vehicles of South Eastern Railway origin, including those built or reconstructed subsequently.
3. Vehicles of South Eastern & Chatham Railway origin built during the Wainwright period, including those wagons acquired secondhand between 1899 and 1913.
4. Vehicles of South Eastern & Chatham Railway origin built during the Maunsell period.

Inevitably, there will be some wagons which do not fit neatly into one of the four categories. Only group 1 is self-contained,

since apart from two LCDR wagons built at Longhedge in 1900, development of the Chatham wagon ceased in 1899. Late SER practice continued into the SECR, owing to the continued influence of Harry S. Wainwright, so there is some overlap between groups 2 and 3. Most acquired wagons come within this period, although the SER had made secondhand purchases in the years before 1899. Wagons reconstructed in the period after 1912 are generally dealt with in the earlier sections, unless the rebuild was extensive enough to be considered as a new wagon, although this was not always how the railway accountants of the period may have recorded matters. The Maunsell period was very different to what had gone before, but again, much rebuilding took place.

However, before we embark on the survey, it is necessary to explain the various brake gear codes which will be used, in particular in the numbering tables throughout the book. These were used in Volumes 1 and 2, but are repeated here for completeness.

SB   Single block and lever one side.
DB   Double block and lever one side.
F   Freighter double block and lever both sides.
M   Morton clutch brake.
SC   Screw brake (on brake vans and bogie vehicles).
AVB   Automatic vacuum brake complete.
SL   Any type of brake with a lever on one side.
ES   Any type of brake with a lever on both sides.
ST   J. Stone's patent brake.
H   Hill's patent either-side brake.
LL   Lift-link brake (SECR Maunsell either-side brake).

The London, Chatham & Dover Railway

This is the only occasion in the entire volume where there were sufficient LCDR wagons to warrant a section of their own. Almost 1,300 vehicles were passed to the SECR in 1899, 60% of the total LCDR wagon stock. They were highly standardised and only six Southern Railway diagrams concern us here. Two of these varied only fractionally in their dimensions, reducing the visible number of types to just five. These are listed below in the order in which we shall consider them.

SR Diagram	SECR Diagram	Vehicle Type	Capacity (Tons)	Length over Headstocks	Wheelbase	Known Period of Construction	Remarks
1326	s1061	Three-plank drop-side (coal and open goods)	6 and 8	15ft 0in	9ft 3in	1873-1900	Ballast wagons were identical (see page 138).
1330 and 1331	s1093	Three-plank open (low)	8 and 10	15ft 0in	9ft 3in	1863-92	1in difference in body depth.
1325	s1092	Four-plank open (medium)	6, 7, 8 and 10	15ft 0in	9ft 3in	1865-99	
1329	s1091	Four-plank open (high)	8 and 10	15ft 0in	9ft 8in	1862-99	Original high open goods.
1332	s1091/1	Four-plank open (high)	8 and 10	15ft 10in	9ft 8in	1875-99	Later high open goods.

All the open goods wagons originally had high round ends, with a slightly different profile to that used by the SER.

Removal of these commenced in 1912, when general reconstruction of the better LCDR vehicles began, but not all vehicles were dealt with before 1923. Brake gear on LCDR stock was seldom more than single or double block, the latter being provided from 1894 onwards. Those vehicles reconstructed by the SECR are thought to have generally received freighter brake gear, but this does not always seem to have been done. Many LCDR wagons were withdrawn in the 1907-12 period and their wheels, springs and axleboxes were reused under 'new' ballast and timber/bolster wagons. The table of statistics reproduced in Appendix 2 will show that the average age of LCDR wagons was somewhat higher than for the SER, so it is possibly not surprising that only 110 open goods wagons remained in ordinary traffic as at 1 January 1923 and some of these were withdrawn before being allocated Southern Railway numbers. Fewer still actually received their allotted numbers. A full list of these may be found in Appendix 1 on pages 158-9.

LC&DR 3 PLANK DROPSIDE WAGON

SR DIAGRAM 1326
BALLAST WAGONS WERE SIMILAR

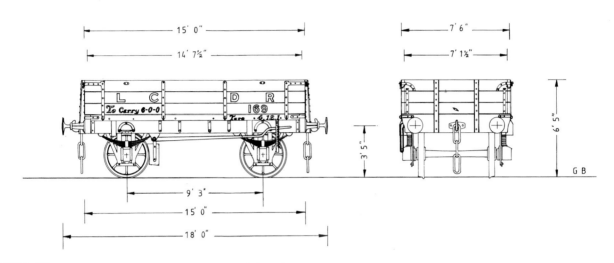

Above:
Figure 3 The LCDR three-plank dropside, described rather unusually as a 'coal and open goods wagon'. The use of a dropside wagon for coal traffic has been noted on only a few railways in this country. These were Nos 1-200 in the LCDR wagon stock list, later SECR Nos 11392-591. Just nine became SR stock as diagram 1326 and the last was withdrawn in August 1927, still numbered as SECR 11521. Sixteen more survived as ballast wagons, LCDR numbers originally being 6001-40, later SECR 11826-65, and the last of these was withdrawn in November 1930.

Left:
Plate 10 Photographs of these wagons are hard to find. SECR No 11517 is seen at Ramsgate, circa 1905. Built in 1883 as LCDR No 126, it ran until 1914 and then became a departmental vehicle. They were a popular choice for crane match trucks, as noted in Chapter 11. *R. W. Kidner Collection*

Below left:
Plate 11 Similar vehicle No 11537, formerly LCDR No 146, at Longhedge, circa 1905. Examples of these wagons which survived to SR days are SECR Nos 11413/29/64, 11521/63/64 and 11826/32/43/58/60-3. Ex-SECR No 11556 was the last LCDR wagon built, in June 1900. Also visible is ex-SER diagram 1327 open No 5253, which was built by Birmingham Railway Carriage & Wagon Co [BRCW] in 1873.
J. Tatchell Collection

Left:

Plate 12 LCDR open goods wagons were divided into three classes: low, medium or high according to the height of the sides. No 875 is a low open goods with three 9in side planks, but some had a 10in bottom plank. This was built as long ago as 1863 by Gloucester Wagon Co. It is untypical in several respects, especially in so far as the iron underframe and livery are concerned. The base colour is black instead of the usual grey and the lettering layout, including the full stops, differs from all other known photographs. No 875 later became SECR No 10768 and was scrapped in 1902. *GRCW Collection*

Below left:

Plate 13 Similar wagon SECR No 10766 at Longhedge, circa 1905. Its former LCDR number was 873. At first glance it appears identical to No 875, but this has a timber underframe so is almost certainly a Longhedge replacement of the original 1863 vehicle, utilising the same body ironwork, and dates from the 1880s. *J. Tatchell Collection*

Below:

Figure 4 The LCDR low open goods, allocated SR diagrams 1330 or 1331 according to side height. The example drawn, LCDR No 730 (later SECR No 10623), was one of those few noted having external diagonal strapping. LCDR numbers of the low open goods wagons all appear to be between 500 and 899.

L C & D R   3   P L A N K   O P E N   W A G O N   (LOW).   8T

S R   D I A G R A M S   1 3 3 0 / 1

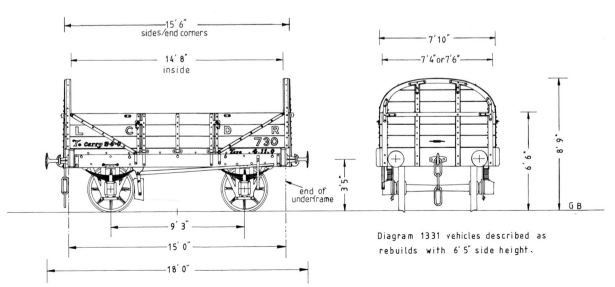

Diagram 1331 vehicles described as rebuilds with 6'5" side height.

Above:
Plate 14 Another LCDR low open goods wagon, SECR No 10756, photographed after rebuilding at Ashford Works on 22 October 1913, as recorded on the left-hand end of the solebar. This began life as LCDR No 863, again built by Gloucester Wagon Co in 1863, almost certainly being identical to No 875 illustrated opposite. This however has been replaced twice: firstly in the 1880s on a timber underframe and then again in 1913, when the round ends were removed and normal steel corner plates replaced the original timber corner posts and end framing. It is not known how many wagons were so extensively rebuilt, or how many simply lost their round ends as a 'reconstruction'. Despite the amount of work carried out on No 10756, it retains a single-block brake on one side only and was still rated at only six tons capacity. The tare weight was recorded as 4 tons 11cwt 3lb. Withdrawal took place in May 1920. The framework in the wagon appears to be destined for a meat van, being typical of the internal arrangements for such vehicles. *SECR Official*

Below:
Figure 5 A drawing of the diagram 1330/31 vehicles, just three of which were allocated SR numbers. These were LCDR Nos 503, 718/81, later SECR Nos 10398, 10611/74. They were finally allocated Southern numbers 14896, 10035/6 respectively. The last survivors were SR Nos 10036, withdrawn in July 1928, and 14896, the 10-ton example, which might have lasted a little longer. All three are recorded as having been 'reconstructed' in 1912/13.

LC & DR 3 PLANK OPEN WAGON (REBUILT SECR)

SR DIAGRAM 1330

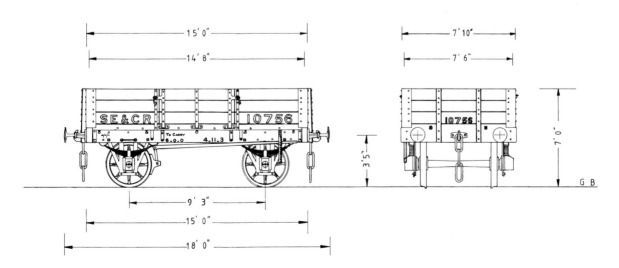

L C & D R 4 PLANK OPEN WAGON MEDIUM 8T

SR DIAGRAM 1325

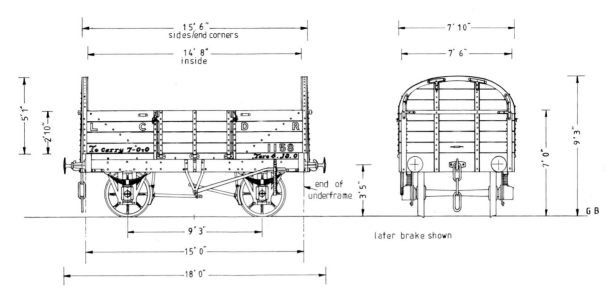

Above:

Figure 6 The LCDR medium open goods wagon had four side planks giving an internal depth of 2ft 10in, usually made up of three 9in planks plus a top plank of 7in width. Some, however, had four 8½ in side planks. The SR diagram was 1325, which states that 28 wagons existed on 1 January 1923, but only 23 were actually allocated Southern numbers. Few of these were renumbered and the last example, SR No 9648, ex-SECR No 10950, was withdrawn in May 1928. Interestingly, this was completed in December 1899, one of the last wagons built at Longhedge. There were 6, 7, 8 and 10-ton versions and some are listed below.

LCDR No	SECR No	SR No	Capacity	LCDR No	SECR No	SR No	Capacity
844	10737	9640	6 tons	672	10567	10024	8 tons
955	10848	9644	7 tons	853	10746	10028	8 tons
982	10875	9645	7 tons	1200	10992	10031	8 tons
1148	10940	9646	7 tons	1246	11038	10033	8 tons
1207	10999	9649	7 tons	601	10496	14569	10 tons
513	10408	10021	8 tons	1121	10913	14570	10 tons

Below:

Figure 7 The LCDR high open goods wagon had an internal depth of 3ft 4in, achieved by the unusual use of four 10in side planks. There were two versions; a 15ft-long type dating from 1862 and a 15ft 10in-long type, built from 1875. The shorter vehicles became SR diagram 1329, which states that only seven were running in 1923. The last of these was withdrawn in 1924, so it seems unlikely that any carried their allocated Southern numbers. Known numbers are: LCDR 537/73/80/88, 635/40, 1114, which became SECR 10432/68/75/83, 10530/5 and 10906 respectively. The solitary 8-tonner in the above list, LCDR No 580/SECR 10475, was the last survivor, being allocated SR departmental stock number 0757S in July 1924. It remained in use as a tunnel inspection truck until 1932.

L C & D R 8 / 10 TON OPEN WAGON (HIGH ENDS)

SR DIAGRAM 1329

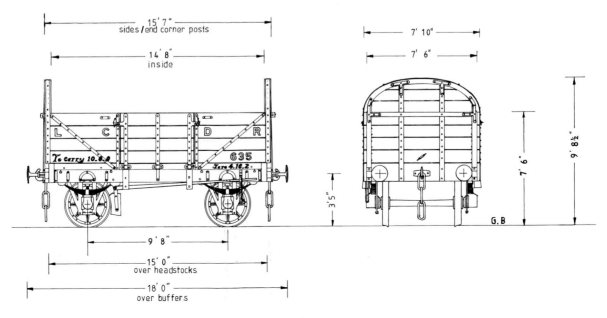

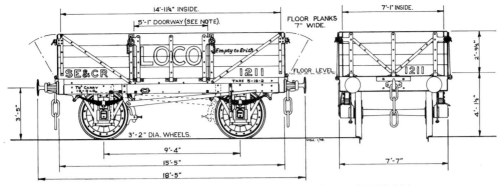

SER 10 TON 4 PLANK LOCOMOTIVE COAL WAGON (CONVERTED).
S. R. DIAGRAM 1342.
NOTE: SIDE DOORS REMOVED IN SECR PERIOD – THROUGH PLANKING SUBSTITUTED.

Above:
Figure 17

Around 1898 or possibly a little earlier, some diagram 1333 wagons were rebuilt with the very unusual feature of a drop-flap door at both ends, for locomotive coal traffic. Perhaps as many as 100 were so modified and the idea may have been to facilitate the end-on coaling of tank engines in restricted locations where it was not possible to provide a normal coal stage; for example, at some suburban termini. The conversion drawing shows the wagons as retaining their side doors but the SR diagram indicates that some, at least, had them through-planked by 1923, although the centre hinge remained in place as a support. Eighty-seven of these wagons remained in traffic at the end of World War 1, but this total had reduced to 43 by 1 January 1923, as stated on SR diagram 1342. Only 32 were allocated SR Nos and the last was withdrawn in July 1935. Few photographs are known, the lettering layout shown above coming from a distant view at Paddock Wood, taken about 1910. Other examples of SECR numbering are 825, 834-6, 873, 888, 903, 1176, 1189, 1201, 1213 and 1226. All those selected for conversion appear to have come from the batches numbered between 825-904 and 1175-274.

In the last five years of the 19th century, the South Eastern experienced a considerable increase in goods traffic. As an interim measure a number of wagons were hired, but over this period some 2,000 new wagons were purchased from rolling stock manufacturers or completed at Ashford Works. Included within these purchases were 1,150 open goods and coal wagons of new design, with a further 100 of similar type completed at Ashford. Construction spanned 1897-1901, so the final batches were amongst the first vehicles to appear in SECR livery; indeed some may have carried the short-lived lettering style of 'SE&CDR' or 'SECDR'. All ran on steel underframes and Wainwright stated in a press article in 1897 that he had now adopted steel underframes generally — a statement certainly not borne out by subsequent events.

Both the open goods and the coal wagons were still 15ft 5in long, with the usual 9ft 4in wheelbase, but for the first time in 'modern' SER history a five-plank side was used. The prototype coal wagon No 2256, described previously, may well have been the first such wagon. The only really obvious difference between the two 1897 designs was that the open goods wagon had the traditional high round end, whilst the coal wagon had the usual low 'D' end and a Williams patent

sheet rail. The coal wagon was in fact described as an 'open goods or coal wagon', thus officially underlining its dual purpose.

Other features new to the South Eastern were eight-spoke wheels of 3ft 1½ in diameter and J. Stone's either-side patent hand brake. This used a left-handed lever on one side of the wagon (ie both levers were at the same end) together with a cross-link which allowed both brake levers to be released simultaneously from either side. The details of this varied over the years and at least three versions were eventually in use.

With no less than four suppliers involved — Ashbury Carriage and Iron Co, Birmingham Railway Carriage and Wagon Co, Oldbury Carriage and Wagon Co plus Ashford Works — there were several variations in detail and by no means all the open goods wagons actually had high round ends, nor were all the coal wagons equipped with 'D' ends or sheet rails. Both steel channel and Fox pressed steel underframes were employed. There is also some evidence of sub-contracting by the various firms involved, so it may prove difficult to determine which constructional features were found on which batch of wagons and exactly who built what!

Left:
Figure 16 The later version of diagram 1334 with five side planks and a 4ft door. One prototype was completed in 1897, described in the order book as 'one new coal wagon', SER No 2256. This was noted as being to SECR diagram s1/1081. Ninety more were built in 1899/1900, but may have differed in detail from the prototype. These were selected for trials with the first version of Hill's either-side brake. An article appeared in *The Engineer* for 11 October 1901, wagon No 2798 being illustrated. Subsequently, the design of brake rack was modified and a further article in January 1903 described the 'production' version. That shown here is the original; for the later style see **Figure 24**.

Left:

Plate 34 One of the 300 Oldbury wagons of 1897, SECR No 8171 is seen at Dover about 1924. This later became SR No 12349 and was one of only 11 examples to diagram 1340 to be dual fitted. As such, it may be in brown livery but this is difficult to judge from the photograph. The whole lot were SECR Nos 7930-8229, later SR Nos 12113-407 and all these did feature high round ends and a Fox pressed steel underframe. The 11 dual-fitted wagons were SECR Nos 8024, 8134/9/40/2/58/65/71/88, 8207/14. *G. P. Keen*

Left:

Plate 35 One of the 300 Ashbury wagons of 1900, SECR No 9567 is seen at Old Oak Common East signalbox about 1924. This later became SR No 12675 and has a steel channel underframe and square ends. Double-block brake gear appears to be provided, in contrast to the Stone's brake on No 8171. Numbering of the complete batch was SECR 9300-599, later SR Nos 12408-707. None were vacuum or dual fitted. *G. P. Keen*

In addition to the above batches, Ashford completed 25 more diagram 1340 wagons in 1900, but as yet no photographs of these have come to light. The exact details of them are thus uncertain, but they probably had pressed steel underframes and high round ends, in true Ashford tradition. Numbers were SECR 2845-69, which later became SR Nos 12088-112. These would have carried SECR livery from new, as did numbers 9300-599.

All these wagons were well built and many lasted until the late 1930s. The last survivor was withdrawn in May 1942, but others could still be found in departmental stock for a few more years. Many of the Oldbury wagons would have lost their round ends after 1912. **Figure 18** on the next page is a combined drawing of both 1897 designs, allocated SR diagram numbers 1340 (open goods) and 1341 (coal wagon). The drawing features the steel channel underframe; the pressed steel version may be found as diagram 1345 on page 52.

Opposite:

Plate 36 Diagram 1341 coal wagon SER No 8639. Possibly the finest photograph of a wagon in SER livery ever taken, although it is actually in photographic grey rather than red livery. The blacked-up body ironwork and the grey running gear are untypical, but the lettering detail is shown to perfection. This is one of the 250 diagram 1341 wagons ordered from Ashbury, but it bears a Birmingham RC&W Co plate, so it seems that Ashbury must have sub-contracted its order. These were SR Nos 8630-879, later SR Nos 13081-330, completed from December 1897 to February 1898. SER No 8639 was later SR No 13090 and ran until June 1933. Stone's brake gear was carried throughout. *BRCW Co*

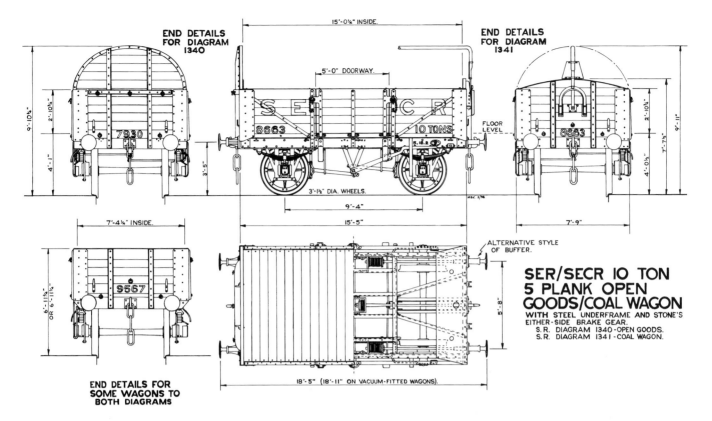

END DETAILS FOR DIAGRAM 1340

15'-0¼" INSIDE.

5'-0" DOORWAY.

S E R

C R

7930

8663

10 TONS

FLOOR LEVEL

END DETAILS FOR DIAGRAM 1341

8663

9'-10¾"

2'-10¾"

4'-1"

3'-5"

3'-1½" DIA. WHEELS.

9'-4"

9'-11"

2'-10¾"

7'-7½"

4'-0½"

7'-4¼" INSIDE.

9567

6'-11¾" OR 6'-11¼"

END DETAILS FOR SOME WAGONS TO BOTH DIAGRAMS

15'-5"

ALTERNATIVE STYLE OF BUFFER.

5'-8"

18'-5" (18'-11" ON VACUUM-FITTED WAGONS).

7'-9"

SER/SECR 10 TON 5 PLANK OPEN GOODS/COAL WAGON
WITH STEEL UNDERFRAME AND STONE'S EITHER-SIDE BRAKE GEAR.
S.R. DIAGRAM 1340 - OPEN GOODS.
S.R. DIAGRAM 1341 - COAL WAGON.

Above:
Figure 18 The 1897-1901 designs of open goods and coal wagons to SR diagrams 1340/41.

Below:
Plate 36 Diagram 1341 coal wagon SER number 8639.
BRCW Co.

SER 8639

To Carry 10.0.0   6.5.0

Right:
Plate 37 Another from the Ashbury/ BRCW batch, SECR No 8663, photographed at an unidentified location around 1924. This shows the left-handed brake lever on the other side, compared with No 8639. It also shows standard Maunsell-era lettering. This wagon was later SR No 13114. Note that the raised 'D' end and sheet rail are absent, perhaps removed subsequent to construction. *G. P. Keen*

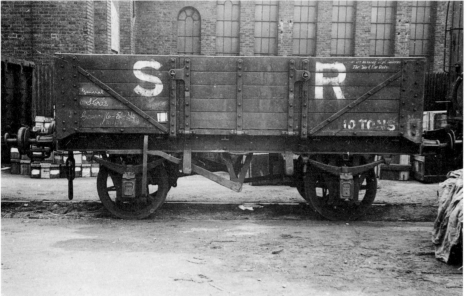

Left and below left:
Plates 38 and 39 Two views of a wagon ordered from Birmingham RC&W Co in SR departmental use at Stewarts Lane in 1936. This started life as SER No 8410 in December 1897 and became SR No 12861 after the Grouping. In February 1930 it was transferred to the loco running department for use at Battersea and was renumbered 463S, finally being withdrawn in April 1938.

The whole batch of 300 carried SER Nos from 8330 to 8629 and were completed over the period November 1897 to February 1898. SR Nos were 12781-3080. This wagon has square ends and no sheet rail so may have been built in this condition rather than being modified subsequently.

The lower photograph is a close-up of the SECR type 'D' axlebox and the left-handed brake lever. However, it does throw up one further mystery. The building plate on the solebar proclaims the Oldbury Carriage & Wagon Company. Did Birmingham RCW Co sub-contract its order as well? Or are the official records incorrect? If so, it will not be the first time! *Both G. Hemingway*

Above:
Plate 40 Ashford's contribution to diagram 1341 is illustrated by No 2900, as built in 1901. This exhibits standard Wainwright lettering, but notice that the tare weight has yet to be painted on the solebar, below the running number. This later became SR No 12712 and ran until 1933. The Ashford wagons to this diagram were numbered SECR 2896-970, later SR Nos 12708-80. All 75 were completed between April and June 1901 using Fox pressed steel underframes. It was these wagons which were built in the open air at Ashford Works, during a period when resources were stretched to their limit. A *Railway Magazine* article at the time extolled the virtues of these Fox underframe 'kits' which allowed such operation to take place, but the reality might have been somewhat different. The kits had originally been designed for export, where it would be likely that assembly might take place in unfavourable locations. Note that the wagon has a sheet rail, 'D' end and somewhat different door hinges compared to the contractor-built examples. J. Stone's brake is provided, the patent plate appearing on the vee hanger. The pressed steel headstocks appear quite different from the steel channel fittings. *SECR Official*

Left:
Plate 41 Evidence that not even all the Ashford wagons were the same is provided by SECR No 2968, at Grove Park in May 1924. This later was SR No 12778 and, by the date of the picture, was running minus 'D' end and sheet rail. Otherwise the wagon appears as SECR 2900, with Fox pressed steel underframe and end uprights. The last diagram 1341 wagon was withdrawn in March 1948, although the majority had gone by 1939. Note the LNWR goods brake van on a regular through working, probably from Willesden via the West London line. *H. C. Casserley, courtesy R. M. Casserley*

43

The South Eastern & Chatham Railway under Wainwright

Because of the continued influence of Harry S. Wainwright, late SER practice continued to become that of the SECR. Some 90 wagons to diagram 1334, 325 to diagram 1340 and 75 to diagram 1341 from the previous section were ordered in the name of the SECR and these appeared during 1899-1901, some possibly being at first lettered 'SE&CDR' or 'SECDR'. Several of the general arrangement drawings of the period are similarly lettered.

Within this section we will deal with those new designs ordered between 1899 and 1913, plus those vehicles acquired secondhand from various sources. The newly formed company found itself short of wagons almost immediately and purchased 750 secondhand open goods and mineral wagons between 1899 and 1902, whilst a further 228 coal wagons were similarly added to stock in 1911-13. Fifteen Southern Railway diagrams concern us here and there are also two acquired types which failed to receive SR diagram numbers in 1923. All are listed below in approximate chronological order.

SR Diagram	SECR Diagram	Vehicle Type	Capacity (tons)	Length over Headstocks	Wheel-base	Known Period of Construction	Remarks
1337	s1088	Five-plank coal	10	15ft 1in	9ft 0in	Psd from E. Griffith 1899/1900	Most later reconstructed.
—	Unknown	Four-plank coal	10	Not recorded, may be variable	Not recorded, may be variable	Psd from Birmingham RC&W Co, 1900	Dumb-buffers For loco coal
—	Unknown	Six-plank coal	8 and 10	Not recorded, may be variable	Not recorded, may be variable	Psd from Metro RC &W Co, 1901/2	Dumb-buffers For loco coal
1352	s1038	Four-plank dropside	10	15ft 0in	9ft 0in	Psd from Price & Reeves, 1901/2	Some to IOW from 1924
1335	s1053	Five-plank coal	10	15ft 5in	9ft 0in	1900-2	With 'D' or square ends
1344	s1068 and s2514/3	Five-plank open	10	15ft 5in	9ft 0in	1900-3	With round ends
1343	s1082	Five-plank open	10	15ft 5in	9ft 0in	1903-7	Some with 'D' ends
1345	s1072	Five-plank open	10	16ft 0in	9ft 0in	1905	With 'D' ends Steel u/frame
1336	s1073	Five-plank open	10	15ft 5in	9ft 0in	1907-8	Square ends
1360	s1035	Eight-plank coal	15	18ft 0in	9ft 9in	1909-10	For loco coal
1353	s1083 or s1833	Six-plank coal (RCH Spec)	10	14ft 11in	9ft 0in	Psd from Bute Works Supply Co & others 1912/13	Different types Most reconstructed from 1916
1354	s1083 or s1833	Six-plank coal (RCH Spec)	10	15ft 11in	9ft 0in	Psd from Bute Works Supply Co & others 1912/13	Different types Most reconstructed from 1916
1350	s2522/5	Six-plank coal	10	16ft 0in	9ft 0in	Reconstructed 1918/19	Ex-diagrams 1353 and 1354
1356	s1034	Seven-plank mineral	12	16ft 6in	9ft 0in	Ex-War Dept 1921	RCH design, no end door
1357	s1034	Seven-plank mineral	12	16ft 6in	9ft 0in	1910-13	RCH design, no end door
1358	s1084	Seven-plank mineral	12	16ft 6in	9ft 0in	1913-14	RCH design, with end door
1359	s1085	Seven-plank open	12	16ft 6in	9ft 9in	1914-15	With top doors

Several wagons included on diagrams 1353 and 1354 were acquired from small firms in the 1912-13 period, notably from a Mr Cornforth (one wagon), Hills Bros of Sevenoaks (four wagons) and High Brooms Brick & Tile Co (15 wagons). In many cases their dimensions were at variance with those noted on the diagrams. In addition, eight coal wagons were acquired from J. & B. Martin in 1911. These were allocated SECR Nos 3254-61 but all had been withdrawn from service before 1923, so did not receive a Southern Railway diagram number.

Inevitably, some of these wagons overlap sections 2 and 4. The diagram 1337 vehicles may have actually received SER livery, but all the others carried SECR livery, in whatever form, from delivery. Diagrams 1353/54 were nominally RCH mineral wagons but from the details on the original general arrangement drawings it is obvious that there were at least six different types of wagon involved, although the SECR allocated just one diagram at first, with a second subsequently added. Similarly, the dumb-buffered coal wagons from Birmingham and Metropolitan in 1900-2 probably included several variants. These were possibly formerly hired out by their respective owners and were already fairly old by the time of purchase. Diagram 1359 could have featured in group 4, and, if truth be told, might be Maunsell's first design for the SECR rather than Wainwright's last. Either way, it is virtually a standard RCH 12-ton coal wagon with the addition of top doors over the drop flap, thereby rendering it suitable for coal or general merchandise.

We will now consider the wagons in detail.

Right:
Plate 42 The first of the 1899-1902 acquisitions were the 50 coal wagons from E. Griffith, SECR Nos 9050-99, purchased in 1899/1900 for the sum of £60 each. They were five-plank coal wagons with a lifting flap over the drop door, which made them suitable for ordinary goods traffic as well. SECR No 9052 was photographed at Bricklayers Arms about 1920. This was one of the 10 survivors at the Grouping and was later allocated SR No 11297. *Authors' Collection*

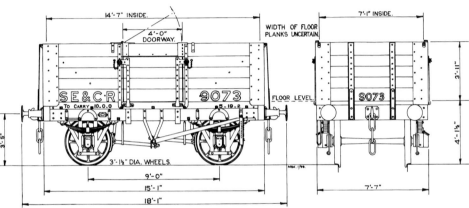

SECR 10 TON 5 PLANK COAL WAGON - EX. E. GRIFFITHS.
RECLASSED BY S.R. AS OPEN GOODS WAGONS. S.R. DIAGRAM 1337.

Left:
Figure 19 A drawing of the E. Griffith wagons to SR diagram 1337. They were reclassified as open goods wagons by the Southern. Most were 'reconstructed' from 1912 onwards, but this does not seem to have altered their appearance at all. The last survivor, SR No 11303, was equipped with freighter brake gear in October 1931 and ran until May 1939.

In 1900-02 600 dumb-buffered coal wagons were purchased, 150 from Birmingham RCW Co (SECR Nos 12071-220) and 450 from Metropolitan Railway Carriage & Wagon Company (MRCW) (SECR Nos 12221-520). All were nominally the same, but in fact most of the BRCW vehicles had six planks, while those from Metropolitan had four. Some of the latter were rated at only 8 tons capacity, but the majority could carry 10 tons. The origin of these wagons is not known but they were probably built for hire and the number of individual variations might have been considerable. All were used for loco coal traffic and were labelled 'Empty to Erith' on the top plank. When delivered, they had blacked-up ironwork but this feature was not perpetuated on subsequent repaints.

Left:
Plate 43 Former MRCW loco coal wagon No 12443 keeps company with a diagram 1327 open at Slade Green, circa 1905. Notice that the diagram 1327 vehicle has also been used for coal traffic, despite its open goods wagon status. *Lens of Sutton*

Plate 44
Left:
Another MRCW wagon, No 12465, is seen when new at Longhedge in 1901. Notice that the end number is placed somewhat higher up than normal, a situation remedied on later repaints. Just one of these wagons survived the Grouping, but was not allocated a Southern diagram. This was SECR No 12433, which had been renumbered as 7889 in 1919, to clear that number range for new stock. It was withdrawn in July 1923 before renumbering as SR 14895. This was not quite the end of the story, as one six-plank wagon survived in a derelict state at Whitstable Harbour into the 1930s, probably as an internal user wagon around the wharves. One further view of wagon No 12404 appears in our title page picture. *LCGB/Ken Nunn Collection*

Right:
Figure 20 One hundred four-plank dropside opens were purchased from contractor Price & Reeves in 1901-2. The design is more typical of railway practice than for a contractor, so it is likely that the contract they were built to serve had a 'sell-on' provision included. SECR Nos were 13021-120 and they were taken into stock in five batches, possibly as stages of the contract were completed. Forty went to France in April 1917 as ballast wagons (WD numbers 26536-75), being returned in 1919/20. They were well built and the SECR classified them as ordinary open goods wagons rather than ballast wagons. The drawing shows them in 'as delivered' condition.

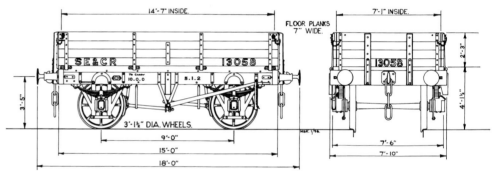

SECR 10 TON DROPSIDE OPEN GOODS - EX PRICE & REEVES.
S.R. DIAGRAM 1352.

Left:
Plate 45 In 1924 18 'Price' wagons again went 'overseas' as ballast wagons, this time to the Isle of Wight. A further two followed in 1931. As SR Nos 62885-904, most survived until 1967, making them by a considerable margin the oldest SECR open wagons to serve with British Rail. In the interests of Isle of Wight standardisation they were rebuilt at Ryde workshops with ex-LBSCR axleboxes and other fittings. No DS62903 is seen in 1960s grey livery with black numbering patches. It was originally SECR No 13058, SR mainland No 14803, and was shipped to the island in July 1931. SR mainland numbers were 14781-841 and all had been withdrawn by 1934. The last island wagon was No DS62888 (SECR No 13050), withdrawn in 1980 and now in preservation at Haven Street. *A. Blackburn*

In 1899 300 coal wagons were ordered from Hurst Nelson & Co of Motherwell. They were delivered in 1900 in SECR livery as Nos 9600-899, these numbers preceding the block given to former LCDR stock in August 1899 (9900-11980). For the first time a 9ft wheelbase was used, but a return was made to timber underframes, thereby contradicting a press statement made by Harry Wainwright in 1897. The 4ft-wide door also returned, but for the last time. All future opens designed by Wainwright would have 5ft-wide side doors, irrespective of their designated use. It was perhaps this detail which hastened the demise of many of these wagons prior to the Grouping. Ashford Works also built 150 of these wagons in 1900-2, but only 265 out of a total of 450 became SR stock as diagram 1335.

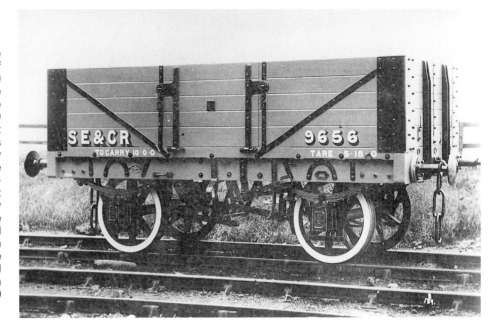

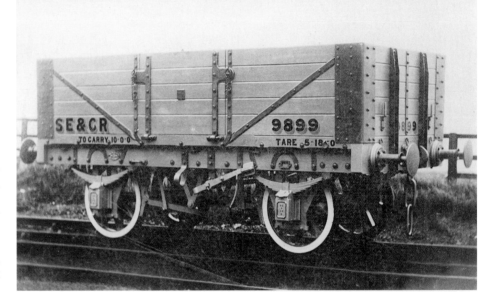

Above right and centre right:
Plates 46 and 47 Two views of the Hurst Nelson wagons. No 9656 is smartly finished in grey with all ironwork blacked-up and the lettering shaded, whilst No 9899, the last of the batch, is in two-tone photographic grey. No 9656 was scrapped before 1923 but No 9899 was allocated SR No 11186 and lasted until July 1926. Both have J. Stone's brake gear, of a different style to that used previously. *Both Hurst Nelson & Co*

Right:
Plate 48 The Ashford-built wagons took random SECR numbers between 2833 and 3386, but had low 'D' ends and a sheet rail. SECR No 3351 is seen, around 1905, at Beckenham Junction. Note the container loaded into the diagram 1344 open behind. No 3351 later became SR No 11029. One more example of the Ashford batch, SECR No 2978, is visible in **Plate 19**.
A. F. Selby

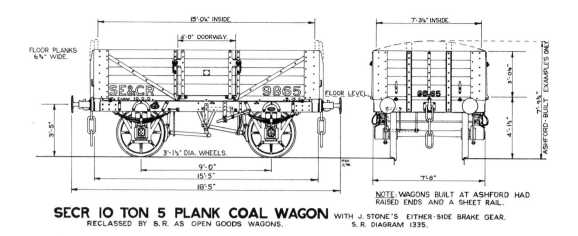

FLOOR PLANKS 6½" WIDE.

15'-0¼" INSIDE.

4'-0" DOORWAY.

SE&CR 9865

FLOOR LEVEL.

3'-5"

3'-1½" DIA. WHEELS.

9'-0"

15'-5"

18'-5"

7'-3¼" INSIDE.

98.65

3'-0¼"

4'-1½"

ASHFORD-BUILT EXAMPLES ONLY.

7'-9¼"

7'-8"

NOTE: WAGONS BUILT AT ASHFORD HAD RAISED ENDS AND A SHEET RAIL.

SECR 10 TON 5 PLANK COAL WAGON WITH J. STONE'S EITHER-SIDE BRAKE GEAR.
RECLASSED BY S.R. AS OPEN GOODS WAGONS. S. R. DIAGRAM 1335.

Above:
Figure 21 A drawing of the five-plank coal wagon to SR diagram 1335. This depicts Hurst Nelson wagon No 9865, which lasted until September 1929 as SR No 11167. The Ashford wagons became SR Nos 10922-1063; those from Hurst Nelson became SR Nos 11064-186. The final survivors were withdrawn in March 1938.

Contemporary with the diagram 1335 coal wagons were the open goods vehicles later to be allocated SR diagram 1344. These shared some of the same features: the 9ft wheelbase, a timber underframe, sometimes with Stone's brake gear and sometimes with Hill's brake gear, but they had a 5ft-wide door and a high round end — the last design to do so. Six hundred were completed, 500 by outside contractors and 100 by Ashford Works. The former had Stone's brake, the latter Hill's brake gear. Again, many failed to become SR stock in 1923, diagram 1344 stating that 221 were in service as at 1 January of that year and only 205 had SR numbers allocated. A possible reason for their early demise could have been the fact that they had inside knees (the 'L'-shaped steel brackets which support the side planks either side of the drop door) and the resulting internal projections might have proved inconvenient when loading the wagons. The various orders issued for the 'reconstructed' diagram 1327 vehicles between 1902 and 1914 stipulated that there should be no internal projections, so external side knees would have been provided. This otherwise almost unnoticeable feature evidently proved a problem to the Goods Traffic Manager. Diagram 1335 also suffered from the same problem, although when used as a coal wagon this would matter not at all.

Numbering details of diagram 1344 are as follows:

SECR Nos	Survivors to SR Nos	Date Built	Brake Gear
3400-49	13782-829	Ashford 1902/3	H
3485-534	13830-78	Ashford 1903	H
12521-820	13879-939	Ashbury 1900-3	ST
12821-3020	13940-86	Hurst Nelson 1901	ST

After withdrawal, the ironwork, wheelsets and other fittings from many wagons were reused on diagram 1347/48/49/51 vehicles between 1916 and 1923, most of which were designated as 'rebuilds'. Some rebuilt from 1916 onwards were allocated SECR diagram s2514/3, having lost the round ends.

SE&CR TO CARRY 10-0-0 13018 TARE 6-4-0

Left:
Plate 49 One of the Hurst Nelson wagons, SECR No 13018 in two-tone photographic grey with shaded lettering but without blacked-up ironwork. The production livery may well have been the same as No 9656 in **Plate 46**. Wagon No 13018 failed to become SR stock, but 13017 did so as No 13986, running until March 1935, probably minus the round ends. *Hurst Nelson & Co*

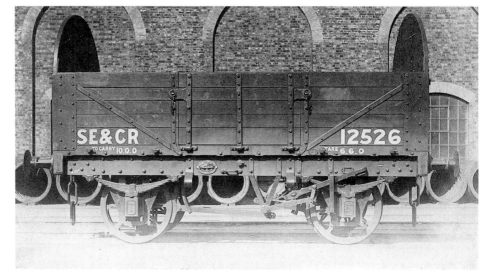

Right:

Plate 50 The Ashbury wagons were much more plainly finished. SECR No 12526 dates from 1900 and was scrapped after a relatively short life in 1918. It exhibits a perfectly executed SECR Wainwright specification lettering layout. On all these wagons the timber solebars were flitched with steel plates. *SECR Official*

Right:

Plate 51 No 3512 was completed at Ashford in October 1903, running until August 1933 as SR No 13856. This has 'Hill's Improved Invicta Patent Brake'. The purpose of the coupling bars is not known; they were probably some form of experimental coupling and uncoupling device designed to obviate the need for the shunters to go between the wagons. The number of accidents caused by this work was considerable. *SECR Official*

Right:

Plate 52 Maunsell livery is carried by SECR No 3448 at Bricklayers Arms in 1920. In this case the wagon still retains an end number. This became SR No 13828. Note how the inside of the round end has been painted only down to the level of the side planking. Behind is diagram 1327 open No 4560, with round ends removed. This was built in 1865 by Brown Marshall. *Authors' Collection*

Almost as the last diagram 1344 vehicles were completed, the design was revised to incorporate outside knees, removing all internal projections. The result was diagram 1343, almost identical in dimensions but having a square or low 'D'-shaped end; 420 of these were built between December 1903 and June 1907, all at Ashford. There were a few detail variations but all appear to have been provided with Hill's either-side brake gear. Twenty utilised McCord's spiral bearing springs (see

Volume 1, Plate 38) in 1906/7, instead of the more usual leaf springs, whilst a few had somewhat unusual Hill's patent sheet supports, as seen opposite in Plate 54.

Below:
Figure 22 Details of the diagram 1343 wagons and the dimensionally similar diagram 1344.

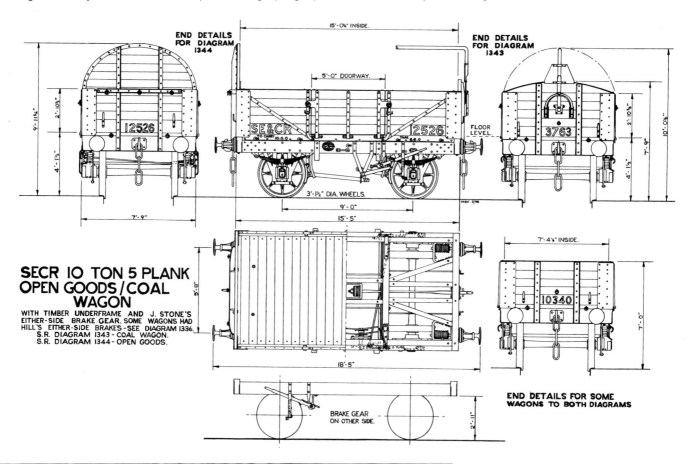

SECR IO TON 5 PLANK
OPEN GOODS/COAL
WAGON
WITH TIMBER UNDERFRAME AND J. STONE'S EITHER-SIDE BRAKE GEAR. SOME WAGONS HAD HILL'S EITHER-SIDE BRAKES - SEE DIAGRAM 1336.
S.R. DIAGRAM 1343 - COAL WAGON.
S.R. DIAGRAM 1344 - OPEN GOODS.

Left:
Plate 53 A square-ended wagon to diagram 1343, SECR No 3607, seen at Ashford in September 1924. This was one of a batch of 100 completed in 1905/6. It is uncertain if it had a low 'D' end when built but according to the official records a sheet rail was originally provided. By 1924 it was boarded for tarred stone traffic only. The later SR number was 13394 and it remained in service until July 1937. Hill's brake gear was fitted. *F. J. Agar*

Above:

Plate 54 Diagram 1343 open goods wagon SECR No 5045, photographed outside Ashford Works after the fitting of the 'Improved Invicta Brake to Hill's Patent' in April 1909. The newly-painted brake lever and rack are clearly seen. Also fitted at the same time were the rather unusual 'Hill's Patent Sheet Supports'. The wagon dates from January 1907 and was part of a batch of 120 completed between October 1906 and August 1907. Presumably this was its first overhaul from new. The later SR number was 13672. SECR numbers of these vehicles were widely scattered, so some examples are given. *SECR Official*

SECR Nos	SR Nos	Date Built	SECR Nos	SR Nos	Date Built
3388-97	13363-72	1905/6	5039-49	13666-76	1906/7
3596-611	13383-98	1905/6	5289-308	13687-706	1907
3630-65	13413-48	1903/4	*10543/61-3/	13758-64	1906/7
3745-92	13525-72	1904/5	5/8/72		
4914-32	13647-65	1906	*With McCord's spiral springs.		

51

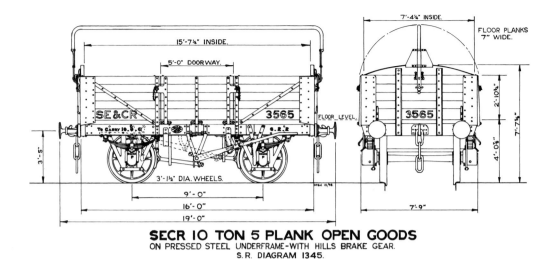

SECR 10 TON 5 PLANK OPEN GOODS
ON PRESSED STEEL UNDERFRAME-WITH HILLS BRAKE GEAR.
S.R. DIAGRAM 1345.

Above:
Figure 23 Whilst the diagram 1343 wagons were being built, one small batch of 50 open goods wagons was completed at Ashford in 1905, using Fox pressed steel underframes. In general appearance they resembled the diagram 1341 vehicles of 1897, having a low 'D' end and a Williams patent sheet rail, but were 16ft long. Hill's brake gear was provided. SECR Nos were 3545-72/4-95, of which all except 3588 survived to become SR Nos 13987-14035, diagram 1345 being allocated. Despite the fact that they lasted until the late 1930s, no photographs are known. The final survivor was SR No 14017, withdrawn in September 1938. The above drawing is based on the details given by general arrangement drawing No 2165.

On completion of diagram 1343, Wainwright produced his final five-plank design. This was almost identical to its predecessor, except that it had square ends and no sheet rail. It was described as an open wagon for both coal and goods traffic, so the decision had finally been taken to cease the construction of separate designs; 110 were completed, in two batches, and all lasted to become Southern Railway stock at the Grouping, being allocated diagram 1336. SECR numbers are fragmented, so examples only are given below.

Sample SECR Nos	SR Nos	Date Built	Brake Gear	Wheels
6012/15-20/8-34/63-70/2-5	11223-72	12/07-2/08	H	3ft 2in Mansell
3387/99, 3822/3, 4900-13, 10416	11187-222	6/08-12/08	H	3ft 1½ in spoke
10425-7, 10604/12-14/30/4	and 11273-96			

All were built at Ashford Works. The last was withdrawn in September 1946.

Below:
Figure 24 Details of Wainwright's final five-plank wagons. Apart from a few 'reconstructions' to diagram 1327 these were the last of the SER/SECR four and five-plank family of designs, the origins of which may be traced back over a period of 45 years.

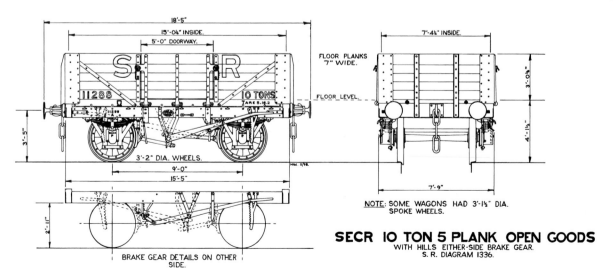

NOTE: SOME WAGONS HAD 3'-1½" DIA.
SPOKE WHEELS.

SECR 10 TON 5 PLANK OPEN GOODS
WITH HILLS EITHER-SIDE BRAKE GEAR.
S.R. DIAGRAM 1336.

BRAKE GEAR DETAILS ON OTHER
SIDE.

Above:

Plates 55 and 56 Two views of diagram 1336 open SECR No 10614, well laden with 29 pockets of hops at Bricklayers Arms, circa 1910. These photographs were taken as part of a series to illustrate a book about the running of a large goods station, but they were equally useful for training employees in the methods of loading the wagons. **Plate 21** was another in the series. The load above is another example that would have been protected by a tarpaulin thrown over the top and secured at solebar level. Wagon No 10614 was completed in December 1908 and later became SR No 11288, the subject of **Figure 24**. Despite the official version of events, the wheels are Mansell rather than spoke! The brake gear is also provided on one side only, later duplicated on the other side. The original cost was recorded as £92 18s 0d and the wagon remained in service until April 1937. These wagons lasted well and most received their allocated SR number and livery. Several may have also carried post-1936 lettering, with the small company initials. *SECR Official*

Below:

Plate 57 Diagram 1336 open goods wagon SR No 11255 at Guildford in 1931. This is one of very few known photographs of Wainwright four or five-plank open wagons in SR livery. Built in 1907 as SECR No 6055, this has Mansell wheels and Hill's either-side brake gear. *E. J. Rose*

As we have now reached a turning point in the Wainwright period, some wagon statistics may be of interest. Two surveys, of wagon brake gear and tarpaulin sheet supports, were undertaken in 1910, the results of each being passed to the General Manager in May of that year.

Sheet Supports

430 wagons — 15ft 5in long. Built 1902-7. 'New pattern sheet supports'.
50 wagons — 16ft 0in long. Built 1905. 'New pattern sheet supports'.
725 wagons — 15ft 5in long. Built 1897-1902. 'Old pattern sheet supports'.

In April 1914 a further addendum was made, stating that the above totals had reduced by eight, three and 184 wagons respectively. These wagons were now running without their sheet supports. The very old timber sheet rails were ignored.

Brake position, 3 May 1910

Total stock of wagons 10939.

Hill's either-side double brakes	710
Stone's either-side double brakes	2,025
Single-lever, double brake (standard PO type)	1,388
Single-lever, single brake	6,816
Total	10,939
	Signed H. S. Wainwright

As will be seen, even as late at 1910 the majority of wagons were still only equipped with a single-block brake on one side only. Board of Trade regulations were starting to come into effect at this time and it would be obligatory to provide either-side brakes on new wagons from November 1911. However, the rules applying to existing stock were less exacting and various extensions of time were granted, giving railway companies until January 1939 to fit all wagons with either-side brake gear of an approved type.

We must now turn to the wagons completed or purchased during the last five years of Wainwright's period of office. These were very different to what had gone before. All were somewhat larger and, in many instances, were to Railway Clearing House (RCH) specification, being purchased from rolling stock manufacturers or secondhand from various other sources. It was during this period that Wainwright came under severe pressure from the directors for, amongst other matters, failing to complete the closure of the workshops at Longhedge. However, it is difficult to understand why such a move was forced through when it was obvious that workshop space at Ashford was at a premium.

Below:

Plate 58 In the early years of the 20th century most British railways experimented with wagons of higher capacity. This was the SECR contribution to the movement. Sixty 15-ton eight-plank mineral wagons were built in 1909 and 1910, in two batches. When first delivered they were lettered '15 TONS COAL WAGON' along the top plank, and were also marked 'Empty to Erith', probably using the same italic script as on the dumb-buffered coal wagons of 1901/2. SECR Nos were 6121-40/97-6211/13-22/8-42 and all except number 6123 became SR stock as numbers 18669-727. SR diagram 1360 was allocated. No 6210 is seen at Ashford in 1924, carrying the standard Maunsell-style livery. It later became SR No 18699. The missing wagon, SECR No 6123, became a crane test weight truck before 1923 and later became SR departmental No 193S. *G. P. Keen*

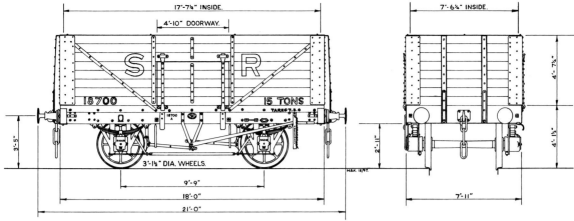

SECR 15 TON 8 PLANK MINERAL WAGON
S.R. DIAGRAM 1360.

Above:

Figure 25 A drawing of the 15-ton mineral wagon, to SR diagram 1360, showing the usual SR 1930s lettering layout. Freighter brake gear was provided on these wagons. A few were cut down to three or four-planks high in SR days, being converted into crane test weight trucks for the outdoor machinery department (ODM). Their heavily constructed underframe, with tiebars between the axleboxes made them instantly recognisable. Five remained in normal service in September 1946 and the last (SR No 18682) was taken out of traffic in March 1950.

In 1912/13 200 coal wagons were purchased secondhand from the Bute Supply Co in South Wales. These were nominally RCH six-plank mineral wagons built in 1900, but in fact there were several different types. For some reason, they were numbered in a duplicate series, with the prefix 'A'. Several other wagons were also purchased at the same time from various other organisations. No photographs of any of these have so far been traced, the drawing below being based solely on the surviving general arrangement drawings. The SECR originally placed them all on one diagram (s1083), but later issued diagram s1833 to cover at least one other version. The Southern placed most of them on diagram 1353 (14ft 11in over headstocks) or 1354 (15ft 11in over headstocks). Twenty rebuilds of 1918/19, without end door, were allocated to diagram 1350. **Figure 26** gives details of the three SR diagrams. Many were 'reconstructed' from 1916 onwards, to a greater or lesser degree.

Below:

Figure 26 SR diagrams 1350, 1353 and 1354.

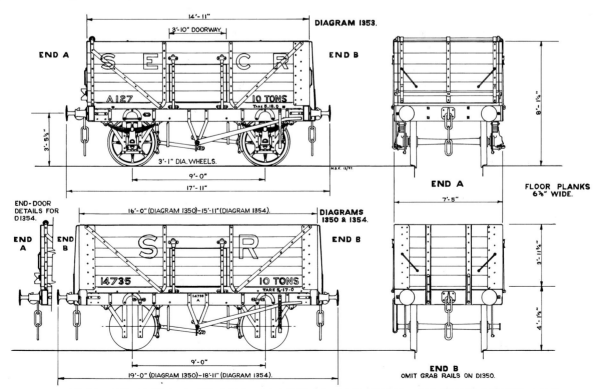

SECR 10 TON 6 PLANK MINERAL WAGONS - EX. BUTE SUPPLY CO.
AS RECONSTRUCTED 1916-1920.   S.R. DIAGRAMS 1350, 1353 & 1354.

SECR general arrangement drawing number A4775 gives the following particulars of the 'Bute Co' wagons, before their reconstruction:

Quantity	Length Outside	Width Outside	Depth Inside	Capacity (tons)	Remarks
131	14ft 11in	7ft 5in	3ft 11¾ in	10	Ex-Bute Supply Co
63	15ft 11in	7ft 5in	3ft 11¾ in	10	Ex-Bute Supply Co
1	14ft 5in	7ft 5in	3ft 11¾ in	10	Ex-Bute Supply Co
5	15ft 5in	7ft 5in	3ft 11¾ in	10	Ex-Bute Supply Co
1	14ft 11in	7ft 5in	3ft 8in	10	Ex-Hills Brothers
2	15ft 11in	7ft 5in	3ft 8in	10	Ex-Hills Brothers
1	15ft 5in	7ft 5in	3ft 10in	10	Ex-Hills Brothers
1	14ft 11in	7ft 5in	2ft 10½ in	8	Ex-Mr Cornforth
205 total					

The authors are of the opinion that the origins of the wagons are as given in the remarks column, although this information was not included on the original drawing. Wagon Nos A1-A200 were allocated to the 'Bute' wagons, A201 to that from Mr Cornforth and A202-5 to those from Hills Brothers of Sevenoaks, but the exact order of numbering is not known.

Fifteen more wagons were purchased from High Brooms Brick & Tile Co in 1913, being allocated SECR Nos A206-20. These again were certainly not all identical. Most wagons kept their original numbers on reconstruction, the exceptions to this being the 20 to diagram 1350, which were reallocated SECR Nos 12101-20.

Examples of SECR numbering are:
Diagram 1353 — A3/9/23/51/98/117/27/79/220
Diagram 1354 — A10/34/66/121/203
SR numbering details may be found in Appendix 1 on page 158.

The last survivors were withdrawn between 1949 and 1951, although the majority had gone many years earlier. SR Nos 14724 and 14730 to diagram 1350 and 14867 to diagram 1353 were among the final survivors.

Above:
Plate 59 This view of Snowdown Colliery, taken in 1913, is of interest for the variety of wagons on view. From left to right they are:

1. Unidentified, possibly diagram 1353/4
2. Diagram 1334 SECR 444 (SR 10539)
3. Diagram 1357 SECR 13254 (SR 16620)
4. Diagram 1341 SECR 8801 (SR 13252)
5. Diagram 1334 SECR 2706 (SR 10857)
6. Diagram 1357 SECR 13738 (SR 17032)
7. Midland Railway open

Number 13254 is lettered '12 TONS COAL WAGON' across the top plank. *G. R. Stenner Collection*

Development of the Kent coalfield began in the early years of the 20th century. Coal was discovered at Shakespeare Cliff during trial borings for the first Channel Tunnel scheme in 1897 and a small amount of coal was raised at this location. Many shafts were then sunk at other locations but only four collieries ever produced worthwhile amounts of coal. The promoters predicted a great future for Kent coal, but it never really achieved all expectations. To cater for the expected increase in traffic the SECR began to order large numbers of 12-ton RCH mineral wagons, no less than 1850 being placed in traffic between 1910 and 1914. Four suppliers were involved: Hurst Nelson, Charles Roberts, R. Y. Pickering and Metropolitan RCW Co. There were minor differences between the various batches but basically only two types of wagon were ordered — those without an end door (SR diagram 1357) and those with an end door (SR diagram 1358). Many of these wagons were purchased in an agreement with the coal factor William Cory & Son, whose wharf on the Thames at Erith gave the SECR so much traffic. It appears that all 500 wagons to diagram 1358 and at least 350 to diagram 1357 were purchased for their use. Nine hundred were rounded up from all corners of the kingdom in 1917/18 to be sent to France (WD Nos being 98501-9400). Ten failed to return in 1921 and so the War Department offered the 10 diagram 1356 vehicles as replacements. They were 2in narrower, hence their different diagram. The SECR however included these on the same diagram as all the other wagons without an end door. Details of numbering are as follows:

SR Diagram	SECR Nos	Survivors to SR Nos	Date Built	Remarks
1356	10551-60	16516-25	Central Wagon Co 1918	Ex-WD Nos 82170-9
1357	13141-340}	SR traffic	{Metropolitan 1910	Lettered '12 TONS COAL WAGON'
1357	13341-440}	dept Nos	{Hurst Nelson 1910	
1357	13441-540}	16526-7667	{R. Y. Pickering 1910	For William Cory & Son
1357	13541-890}	and loco coal	{Hurst Nelson 1911/12	Some for William Cory & Son
1357	13891-990}	Nos 63751-	{C. Roberts 1912/13	For William Cory & Son
1357	14091-590}	63950	{Hurst Nelson 1913	
1358	14591-5090	17668-8166	R. Y. Pickering 1913/14	For William Cory & Son

Mr K. Werrett recorded wagon No 13785 from the Hurst Nelson 1911/12 batches as being plated 'This wagon is loaned for use of LNW Co & must be returned to LNW Line'. The plate was affixed over the wagon number, but the vehicle was otherwise in standard SECR livery. The date was 1920. No further information is available and it is not known how many were on hire to the LNWR.

Despite the failure of the Kent coalfield to achieve its full potential, gainful employment was found for all these wagons. William Cory & Son was a very large company which at one time owned some 5,000 wagons and had a large share of the coal trade in the Southeast. Its business relationship with the SECR concerning these wagons is not clear, but it seems either the SECR purchased them on behalf of William Cory, or purchased them new from William Cory to carry their traffic. An aerial photograph of its wharf at Erith in early SR days shows the vast majority of the many wagons present to be in either SECR or SR livery. From this evidence it appears that Cory's phased out its own Kent area fleet in favour of those provided by the SECR. The following photographs will show that the wagons were not necessarily confined to Kent, but could wander far and wide across the country.

General withdrawal commenced as early as 1924 with the majority being taken out of use prior to World War 2. In September 1946 Southern Railway records list just five wagons to diagram 1356, 31 to diagram 1357 and 15 to diagram 1358 still in traffic. A few of these lasted into the 1950s. During the latter part of World War 2, several were supplied to private owners as 'compensation' for their own mineral wagons having been damaged beyond repair in accidents on the Southern Railway. Others were filled solid with concrete for use as tunnel or junction 'blocking wagons' in event of invasion. These had a third axle provided to carry the additional weight.

On the subject of hired wagons, the SECR utilised a batch of Midland Railway five-plank opens during World War 1, numbered in a 'C' prefixed series. The only vehicle so far noted was No C13, painted red oxide but lettered SECR, in 1919. Some others were hired from William Cory about 1921/22, prefixed '0', but no other details are known.

SECR Goods Stock Telegraphic Codes

Description	Code letters
Open wagons	
Non-whole drop sides, common user	A
With whole drop sides, common user	ADS
Single-plank wagons, common user	ASP
Other types including fitted, non-common user	AN
SECR 12-ton	B
SECR 12-ton loco	BL
Covered wagons	
Ordinary, common user	C
Fitted, non-common user	D
SECR meat vans	P
Foreign meat vans	Q
SECR gunpowder vans	E
Foreign gunpowder vans	F
Timber wagons	
SECR ordinary	GO
SECR batten	GB
SECR twin	GT
Foreign ordinary	GOF
Foreign batten	GBF
Foreign twin	GTF

Description	Code letters
Cattle wagons	
SECR unfitted	J
SECR prize cattle	IP
SECR prize cattle with coupee	IPC
SECR vacuum piped	IV
SECR dual piped	ID
Foreign cattle wagons	K
Implement wagons	
SECR trolleys	L
Foreign trolleys	M
Highway vehicle trucks	
SECR	N
Foreign	O
All other types	
Aeroplane trucks,	
Glass wagons, etc	R
Sheets	S
Ropes	T
Binding chains	U
Service vehicles	S
Goods brake	GBV
Ballast brake	BBV
Ballast wagon	EBW
Rail wagon	ERW

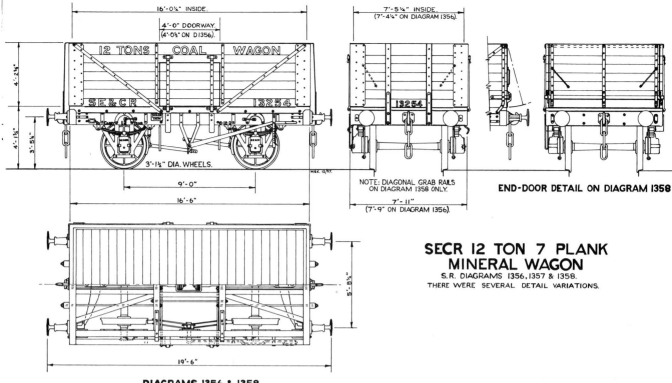

16'-0½" INSIDE.
4'-0" DOORWAY.
(4'-0½" ON D 1356).

12 TONS COAL WAGON
SE&CR 13254

4'-2¼"
4'-1½"
3'-5¾"

3'-1¼" DIA. WHEELS.
9'-0"
16'-6"

7'-5¼" INSIDE.
(7'-4½" ON DIAGRAM 1356).

13254

NOTE: DIAGONAL GRAB RAILS ON DIAGRAM 1358 ONLY.
7'-11"
(7'-9" ON DIAGRAM 1356).

END-DOOR DETAIL ON DIAGRAM 1358

SECR 12 TON 7 PLANK MINERAL WAGON
S.R. DIAGRAMS 1356, 1357 & 1358.
THERE WERE SEVERAL DETAIL VARIATIONS.

5'-8¾"

19'-6"

DIAGRAMS 1356 & 1358.

Above:
Figure 27 A combined drawing of the RCH seven-plank mineral wagons to SR diagrams 1356, 1357 and 1358. This shows the lettering style adopted for the first batch of wagons from Metropolitan in 1910, numbers 13141-340 only. Later batches simply had the lettering '12 TONS' over the drop-flap door. A total of 225 identical wagons were built by Hurst Nelson in 1911/12 for the LBSCR; these however were allocated SR diagram 1373, and were illustrated in Volume 2.

Below:
Plate 60 One of the Hurst Nelson wagons of 1911, SECR No 13578 was photographed by the builders. The immaculate paint finish is what we have come to expect from Hurst Nelson, complete with all ironwork in black. This was the livery carried by most of the mineral wagons when new. Recorded cost is £67 15s 0d. According to the records this is one of the many wagons connected with William Cory & Son, but there is no obvious sign of this arrangement on the vehicle. The subsequent SR No was 16897 and it ran until October 1932. *Hurst Nelson & Co*

Right:

Plate 61 R. Y. Pickering wagon No 13540, built in November 1910. The date is just visible on the left-hand end of the solebar, in small italic figures. This later was SR No 63808 in the locomotive coal wagon series. It too features blacked-up body ironwork. Withdrawal came in June 1937. *R. Y. Pickering Ltd*

Right:

Plate 62 Another Hurst Nelson wagon, SECR No 13620, in Maunsell livery and far from home at Penmaenpool on the Cambrian Railway in 1923. Note that subsequent repaints have omitted the black ironwork. This vehicle was allocated SR No 16934 after the Grouping, but was later reallocated loco coal wagon number 63838 in November 1926. Despite this, the wagon was condemned in September 1929 as No 16934. *J. P. Richards*

Right:

Plate 63 SECR No 14374 is seen at Taunton loco shed at an unrecorded date, but probably about 1920-3. This was one of the Hurst Nelson 1913 wagons and was allocated to loco coal use before the Grouping. Later allocated SR No 17480, it was renumbered as SR loco coal wagon 63949 in September 1927, but was returned to 17480 later. This wagon was a late survivor, running until March 1944. *J. Slinn Collection*

Left:
Plate 64 Another Hurst Nelson wagon from the 1913 batch, vehicle No 14517. This one is not branded for loco coal use. The photograph was taken at Ashford about 1924. This was later SR No 17603. Withdrawal date is not known. *G. P. Keen*

Left:
Plate 65 Considering how many diagram 1357/58 wagons were built, photographs of them in SR livery are not easily found. No 17065 was seen at Ramsgate loco shed in August 1927, well laden with locomotive coal. The former SECR No was 13806 and it was built by Hurst Nelson in 1912. Some limited use was made of Kentish coal for locomotive purposes, usually by mixing it with coals from other sources. Although much SECR loco coal traffic was handled in the company's own wagons, some was delivered by the other large coal factor in the Southeast, Messrs Stephenson Clarke Ltd, so this company's wagons would have been an everyday sight on the system.
*H. C. Casserley, courtesy
R. M. Casserley*

Right:
Plate 66 Diagram 1358 end-door mineral wagon No 15090, as built by R. Y. Pickering in 1914, with all ironwork blacked-up. Appropriately it is the last of the batch and later became SR No 18166, surviving until May 1931.
R. Y. Pickering Ltd

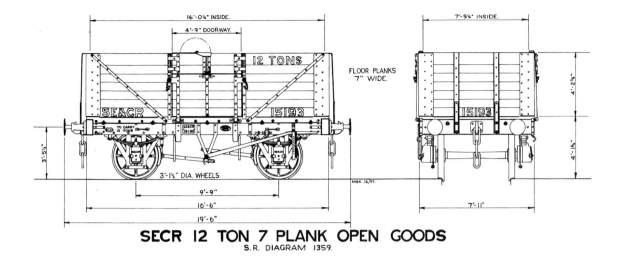

SECR 12 TON 7 PLANK OPEN GOODS
S.R. DIAGRAM 1359.

Above:
Figure 28 What may possibly have been Wainwright's last wagon design for the SECR, although committee minutes of the time record the General Manager as being responsible for the 'RCH' purchases, so perhaps Wainwright was not even consulted about these last wagons. Five hundred 12-ton seven-plank open goods or coal wagons were ordered from Hurst Nelson in 1913. Maunsell had some input into the design, as it is recorded that they were fitted with his patent door fasteners. They were delivered in 1914-15 and cost £87 each.

Right:
Plate 67 The builder's photograph of number 15138 as completed in 1914. They were described as coal wagons by the SECR, but the Southern reclassified them as open goods wagons. The inclusion of top doors allowed them to fit either role. SECR Nos were 15091-590, following on from the diagram 1358 vehicles. Sixty-nine went to France in 1918-20, but all returned to become SR diagram 1359 and running numbers 18167-666 after the Grouping. No 15138 later became SR 18214 and ran until January 1946. *Hurst Nelson & Co*

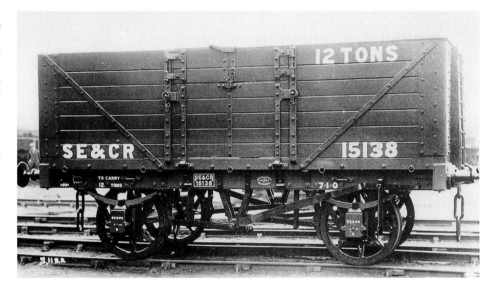

Right:
Plate 68 Taken circa 1921, SECR No 15193 carries Maunsell livery and lettering at Ashford. The date of repaint, '1/12/17' may be seen at the left-hand end of the solebar. The later SR No was 18269. Withdrawal commenced as early as 1928, but the last survivors (SR Nos 18409/60) were not scrapped until February 1950. *G. P. Keen*

The South Eastern & Chatham Railway under Maunsell

Maunsell was most dissatisfied with the situation he found on taking office at Ashford. As far as the open wagons were concerned, some 'reconstructed' diagram 1327 vehicles were still being produced, and there was one outstanding order for the 500 seven-plank coal wagons from Hurst Nelson. Maunsell made some minor revisions to the latter, as recounted in the last section; however, he soon instructed Lionel Lynes, to produce a number of new, much more modern designs. The reorganisation of Ashford Works was pressing and World War 1 prevented much in the way of new construction for the time being. Accordingly, the reconstruction of older wagons had to continue, but production of several 'one-off' prototype wagons was undertaken. Known as 'pattern' wagons, these were put into traffic and thoroughly tested before general production commenced. One seven-plank open wagon was completed in 1915, SECR No 10320, and released to traffic. Two other batches of extensive 'rebuilds' were also completed between 1916 and 1920, on timber underframes, before new construction restarted in earnest, using steel underframes, from 1918 onwards. Just five SR diagrams concern us in this section and they are listed below in approximate chronological order.

SR Diagram	SECR Diagram	Vehicle Type	Capacity (tons)	Length Over Headstocks	Wheelbase	Known Period of Construction	Remarks
1348	s2522/3	Five-plank open	10	16ft 6in	9ft 6in	1916-18	Timber u/frame. 'Rebuild type A'
1351	s2522/4	Five-plank open	10	16ft 6in	9ft 6in	1916-20	Timber u/frame. 'Rebuild type B'
1347	s2522/6	Five-plank open	10	17ft 0in	9ft 6in	1920-5	'Rebuilds'. Fifty with vacuum brakes.
1349	s2522/7	Five-plank open	10	17ft 0in	9ft 6in	1921-2	'Rebuilds'
1355	s2139/2	Seven-plank open	12	17ft 0in	9ft 6in	1915 and 1919-27	One built as a sheep truck, see page 102.

Diagrams 1348 and 1351 were probably stopgaps, only 40 of each type being built. They had one unusual feature for the SECR, namely the use of a Morton-type brake and all are noted as being reconstructed Hurst Nelson wagons, the slight differences in height between the two diagrams resulting from the reuse of available ironwork from different types of wagon.

No photographs of these wagons have been traced, but fortunately the general arrangement drawings have survived and they have been used in the preparation of **Figure 29**, reproduced below.

Ex-SECR numbers are random, so a selection is given below.

SR Diagram	Sample SECR Nos	SR Nos	Remarks
1348	9612/66, 9709, 9816/25/82	14471-510	Replacements for diagram 1335.
1351	12541/678/877/962, 13015	14741-80	Replacements for diagram 1344.

It will be noticed that the SECR numbers are direct replacements for the earlier wagons. Eleven to diagram 1348 and 15 to diagram 1351 remained in traffic in September 1946 and the last ones were withdrawn in 1950.

Below:
Figure 29 SR diagrams 1348 and 1351.

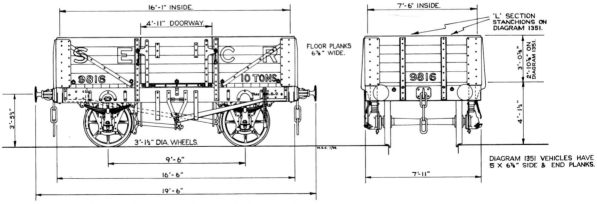

SECR 10 TON 5 PLANK OPEN GOODS (RECONSTRUCTED TYPES A & B).
S.R. DIAGRAMS 1348 (TYPE A - AS DRAWN) & 1351 (TYPE B - AS NOTED).

Above:
Plate 69 Starting in 1920, several batches of 17ft-long five-plank open goods wagons were built. Although described as 'rebuilds', they were in reality almost new wagons, with, possibly, only the wheelsets and buffers as secondhand parts. SECR No 9601 was the first of them, completed by Cravens of Sheffield in April 1920. Two hundred came from this company and the later SR number for 9601 was 14071. It ran until December 1947. SR diagram 1347 was allocated to these wagons. *SECR Official*

Another wagon from the Cravens order, SECR No 9821, appears in **Plate 9**. Perhaps because they were described as rebuilds, most of these wagons were allocated widely scattered numbers in the SECR list. Many were nominal rebuilds of 'Bute Company' and Hurst Nelson diagram 1335 and 1344 vehicles. No 'pattern' wagon appears to have been completed, possibly because there was not much to go wrong when designing a five-plank open wagon. The standardised steel underframe had undergone trials under seven-plank open number 10320 since 1915, so had clearly been adequately tested. The most unusual

feature of these wagons was the lack of a crib rail, the ends of the floor planks being exposed. Normal buffers were provided on diagram 1347 but the very similar diagram 1349 vehicles had self-contained buffers, which was the more usual fitting on Lynes SECR-designed wagons. Dimensionally these two types varied in width by only ¾in and it is perhaps a measure of Maunsell's very orderly approach to things that a separate diagram was prepared. This would have been somewhat unlikely in Wainwright's time. Diagram 1349 also took numbers formerly allocated to LCDR stock.

Below:
Figure 30 A drawing showing both versions of 17ft open wagon to diagrams 1347 and 1349. Also shown are details of the standardised steel underframe as used on most of the Maunsell/Lynes SECR wagons. Note that the drawgear is non-continuous and pulls on the middle cross-bearers. Standard British channel and angle sections are used throughout. This was one of the first wagon designs to use them.

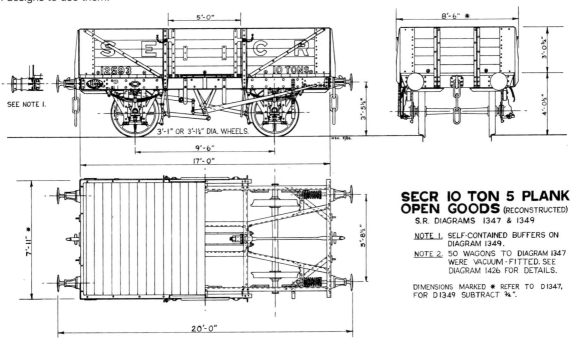

SECR 10 TON 5 PLANK OPEN GOODS (RECONSTRUCTED)
S.R. DIAGRAMS 1347 & 1349

NOTE 1. SELF-CONTAINED BUFFERS ON DIAGRAM 1349.

NOTE 2. 50 WAGONS TO DIAGRAM 1347 WERE VACUUM-FITTED. SEE DIAGRAM 1426 FOR DETAILS.

DIMENSIONS MARKED ✱ REFER TO D1347, FOR D1349 SUBTRACT ¾".

Left:

Plate 70 Fifty wagons to diagram 1347 were vacuum fitted and were boarded 'To work between London, Folkestone & Dover only'. SECR No 9688 was one, photographed at Dover in 1924. It later became SR No 14100. Other fitted examples were SECR Nos 9650/97, 9800/81, 12590, 12605/77 and 12819, later SR Nos 14090, 14104/41/72, 14222/33/79 and 14368. It is not possible to state whether this wagon is in brown or standard grey livery. *G. P. Keen*

Left:

Plate 71 Diagram 1349 wagon No 10789, later SR No 14693. This has self-contained buffers but is otherwise almost identical to diagram 1347. *G. P. Keen*

Opposite:

Plate 74 Diagram 1347 wagon No S14271, pictured in one of an official series of photographs taken at Ashford Works in 1948/9. These wagons were fully repainted in SR brown but had the company initials replaced by the 'S' prefix to the number. At this date full repaints for wagons were becoming rare. This wagon was built in 1923 to an outstanding SECR order. *National Railway Museum*

Left:

Plate 72 A diagram 1347 wagon in SR pre-1936 livery at Stratford, GER, about 1936, No 14131. Because of the lack of a crib rail the tare weight appears on the solebar, unusual for SR practice. The former SECR No was 9778 and this was another Cravens wagon of 1921. It ran until February 1948. Being modern wagons, they survived well and a few lasted to the early 1960s. *G. Hemingway*

Right:

Plate 73 SR post-1936 lettering is carried by No 14283, at Renfrew in May 1947. Built as SECR No 12687 in 1922, it remained in traffic until 1957. The Maunsell/Lynes SECR either-side or lift-link brake was the usual gear for all these wagons, with two brake blocks for unfitted vehicles, four on vacuum-braked stock. Examples of SECR numbering of unfitted diagram 1347 wagons are: 9616-20/42-5, 9891, 12521-3/37-40, 12601-4/57-65, 12736-46, 12853-6, 12921-6/95, 13019. *A. G. Ellis*

Below:

Plate 75 Another Ashford 1948 photograph, this time of diagram 1349 wagon No S14590. Note the addition of steel plates over the exposed floor planks. This was formerly SECR No 10660 and dates from July 1921, being built at Ashford Works. SECR numbers for diagram 1349 were: 10640-52/4-70/5-85/93-10701/3-27/47-76/8-10816. *National Railway Museum*

Above:
Plate 76 One of the 50 vacuum-fitted examples to diagram 1347, No S14422 at Ashford in May 1948, exhibiting some patch-painting, although the end result looks fairly acceptable. This was SECR No 12908, completed by Cravens in June 1921. Quite possibly, the vacuum brake gear was added later by the SECR, especially as the numbers for these vehicles are scattered through the list. Note also the tiebar between the axleboxes, a feature of all the fitted wagons. For details of the brake gear refer to diagram 1426 on page 87. The Southern completed an outstanding SECR order for these wagons, SR numbers being 14401-70 and built 150 more in 1925, SR numbers being 19079-228 (SR order A15). *National Railway Museum*

Left:
Plate 77 A close-up of the SECR No 2 axlebox as used under most of the Maunsell/Lynes 10 and 12-ton wagons in the 1915-26 period. This is actually under a diagram 1744 ballast wagon but may be regarded as typical. The photograph was taken at Lingfield in 1969. *E. R. Kemp*

Above:

Plate 78 The 'pattern' wagon to diagram 1355, SECR No 10320, was lost in traffic by the time that an official photograph was required. General construction of seven-plank open wagons started in 1919, 2,120 more vehicles being completed by 1927, making these the most numerous SECR wagon during the post-Grouping period. No 12221 was photographed in March 1919 and appears to be in all-over grey livery, including the running gear, as favoured by Swindon. Note again the absence of a crib rail. This wagon later became SR No 15698 and it lasted to the 1950s, as did many of these wagons. Some were sold out of service to the Port of Bristol Authority and several of these have since passed into preservation, as have a few diagram 1347 vehicles. A census in January 1961 revealed 71 still in ordinary traffic. None of these wagons had vacuum brakes.
SECR Official

Selected Numbering Details for Diagram 1355

SECR Nos	SR Nos	Date Built	SECR Nos	SR Nos	Date Built
10320	15597	Ashford 1915	Between 20 and 407	14897–14996	Ashford 1923
*12121-500	15598-977	Ashford 1919/20	Between 5210 and 7447	14997–5596	Ashford 1920/1
15791-6090	15978-6277	Cravens 1921	None	28501-9000	Ashford 1926-7
16191-430	16278-398, 18667/8,	Ashford 1922			(SR Order A28-part)
	16399-515				

*Number 12121 was built as a convertible sheep wagon (see **Plate 136**).
It is not known why nos 18667/8 were renumbered out-of-sequence.

67

Right:
Plate 79 One of the SR-built examples to diagram 1355, No 28875, seen at Renfrew in September 1946, freshly uprated to 13 tons. The SR batch all had Williams patent sheet rails and most wagons retained them to the end. *A. G. Ellis*

Right:
Plate 80 No S16510 was photographed ex-works at Ashford in April 1948. Built in 1922 as SECR No 16425, it ran until at least 1958. The SECR oval numberplate has been turned over and the new SR number painted on, with the suffix 'A' for Ashford. *National Railway Museum*

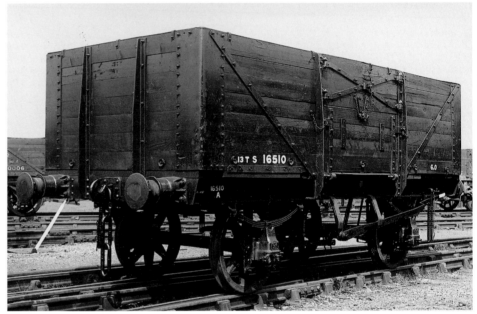

Below:
Figure 31 The Maunsell/Lynes seven-plank open goods wagon to SR diagram 1355. There appear to be very few detail differences among the 2,121 examples to this diagram.

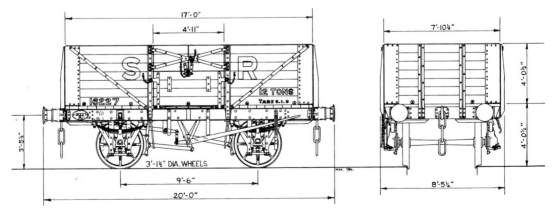

SECR 12 TON 7 PLANK OPEN GOODS
S.R. DIAGRAM 1355
NOTE. SOME WAGONS ARE EQUIPPED WITH WILLIAMS PATENT SHEET RAILS.

Above:
Plate 81 No S28951 at Ashford in April 1948, still retaining its sheet rail. This was built in 1927 for the sum of £167. It ran until at least 1965, serving as a cable wagon in the final years. *National Railway Museum*

Right:
Plate 82 Another wagon from the SR 1926 order, No S28885 is seen at Offord & Buckden (GNR) in April 1952. When photographed, it was still in SR brown livery. This shows the lift-link brake lever. *A. E. West*

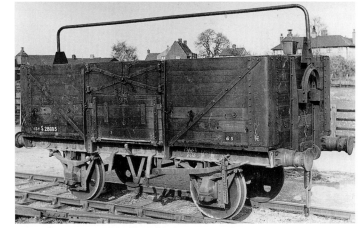

Right:
Plate 83 Completed in February 1927, No S28901 is seen in BR unpainted livery with black number patches, at Teignmouth, Devon, in 1957. The appearance is typical of the final survivors. Some 1,652 wagons were still in traffic in September 1946 but most were withdrawn in the mid-1950s. No DS28635 was seen at Portsmouth in 1970, being one of the last to survive. *D. J. Wigley*

Chapter 4.
Covered Goods Wagons

After open goods and mineral wagons, covered goods vehicles were easily the next largest class of wagon on the SECR, with over 1,300 examples extant at the Grouping. This represented 11% of the total wagon stock, a fairly low proportion when compared to the then national average of around 20%, but far in excess of its nearest neighbour, the LBSCR, which could not even muster 6%. Various possible explanations present themselves, but, quite simply, the company could meet the needs of its customers without constructing large numbers of covered vehicles. The use of tarpaulin sheets in conjunction with the fleet of round-ended open goods wagons was sufficient for most needs. Certainly there were very few fitted wagons or those specifically for perishable traffic.

For the purpose of study, the vehicles will be considered in two groups, as follows:
1. Ordinary covered goods wagons for general merchandise, etc.
2. Ventilated covered goods wagons for fruit, fish, meat and other perishable traffic.

With one exception, group 1 is self-contained. However, group 2 includes some overlap with livestock vehicles, one type being described and illustrated in Chapter 5; this group also includes a passenger-rated design which was actually reclassified and renumbered in the passenger van series by the Southern Railway in 1923.

Ordinary Covered Goods Wagons

Despite the statements made opposite, several of these vehicles were afforded passenger-rated running gear and, in some cases, vacuum and/or Westinghouse brakes in just the same manner as a small number of open goods wagons were equipped for running in 'Express goods trains'. In general, neither the SECR nor the Southern Railway diagrams differentiate between the provision or non-provision of these fittings, both merely confining themselves to internal dimensions and carrying capacities. Consequently, most of the SR diagrams include both fitted and unfitted wagons on the same page. Nine Southern Railway diagrams concern us here and these are listed below in approximate chronological order.

SR Diagram	SECR Diagram	Origin	Capacity (tons)	Length over Headstocks	Wheel-base	Known Period of Construction	Remarks
1419	s1087	SER	6 and 8	14ft 7½in	8ft 0in	1863-80	Originally 125 to this design.
1421	s1086	SER	8	15ft 7in	9ft 0in	1877-81	Originally 110 to this design (see note 2).
1423	s1046	LCDR	8 and 10	16ft 0in	9ft 3in	1875-92	At least 2 with Westinghouse pipes.
1420	s897	SER	8 and 10	15ft 5in	9ft 4in	1889-1900	Originally 278 to this design.
1422	s1067	SER	8 and 10	15ft 5in	9ft 0in	1886 and 1898-1902	Originally 330 to this design (see note 2).
1424	s1052	SECR	8 and 10	16ft 0in	9ft 0in	1904-8	Originally 110 to this design.
1425	s473 and s473A	SECR	10	17ft 0in	9ft 6in	1909-14	Originally 98 to this design.
1426	s2139/1	SECR	10	17ft 0in	9ft 6in	1918-22 and 1925/6	Originally 401 to this design. Some built by SR.
1427	s2139/1	SECR	10	17ft 0in	9ft 6in	Converted in 1923	Ex-diagram 1426, with ventilators. Only six vehicles.

Notes
1. Many LCDR wagons were reconstructed at Ashford Works between 1912 and 1918. There were at least 415 LCDR covered goods wagons in service in 1899, a few being 15ft 0in long, dating from the 1867-75 period.
2. The 10 examples to diagram 1422 completed in 1886 were originally allocated diagram 1421 at the Grouping and may vary dimensionally from later construction.
3. Some examples to diagrams 1420, 1422, 1425, 1426 and all six vehicles to diagram 1427 were vacuum fitted. Some examples to diagram 1425 had dual brakes, ie both vacuum and Westinghouse gear. These were to SECR diagram s473A.

Constructionally, the designs may be grouped into three periods by certain characteristics, irrespective of their origins. All vehicles built up to World War 1 exhibited stout external timber-framed sides, whilst SER diagrams 1419 and 1421, plus all the LCDR stock, had similarly constructed ends. Commencing in 1886, a change was made to a flush-planked end, with either two timber or angle-iron uprights. This gave a slight increase in internal length (and therefore increased cubic capacity) without a corresponding increase in body length. Diagrams 1420, 1422 and 1424 all follow this style. Diagram 1425 does not fit neatly into this or the Maunsell era, despite having external timber body framing on both sides and ends. This diagram featured a three-part door, ie two short cupboard doors over a drop flap, sometimes referred to as a London & North Western pattern door, and in this detail, and in its dimensions, it was the precursor of the Maunsell vehicles; however, beyond these features there was little in common with earlier or later construction.

The Maunsell period is represented by diagrams 1426 and 1427 and these were clearly much more modern than the previous Wainwright designs. Both utilised the standardised Maunsell/Lynes underframe with RCH wheels and they also introduced the distinctive semi-elliptical roof profile which was to become such a characteristic feature of Southern Railway goods vehicles for the next 30 years. It did, however, introduce an unwanted problem — that of leaking roofs! The sight of one of these vans covered with a tarpaulin would become commonplace, as **Plate 84** shows. The reason for the adoption of this profile seems to stem from the desire to achieve a cubic capacity of 1,000ft within the given 17ft body length. Previous designs achieved cubic capacities of between 591 and 891ft, so the additional headroom and width within the roof space of the Maunsell/Lynes design gave the desired result, although whether this was useful in practice is doubtful. However, it does mean that SECR and SR Maunsell vans are easily recognisable in photographs. We will now examine the diagrams in more detail.

Left:
Plate 84 Described by the photographer as an 'up fast goods train', this shows 'D' class 4-4-0 No A732 approaching Bromley South on 15 September 1931 with a fitted goods service from either Folkestone Harbour or Dover Marine to Victoria or Stewarts Lane via Tonbridge, Otford and Swanley, according to the headcode discs. There is a varied collection of vehicles in the train, including stock from all the 'Big Four' companies. At the head is a Maunsell diagram 1426 covered goods wagon with, presumably, a leaking roof, hence the tarpaulin sheet. This problem beset all those Maunsell goods wagons with this roof profile and it was never satisfactorily cured. Further down the train are several passenger-rated vans and it was not at all unusual to find such a combination in a fully or partially fitted goods train. In later years those wagons with a wheelbase of less than 10ft would be barred from express services, but in 1931 no such restrictions were applied. *H. C. Casserley, courtesy R. M. Casserley*

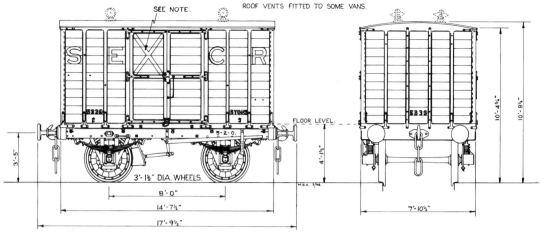

ROOF VENTS FITTED TO SOME VANS.

SEE NOTE.

FLOOR LEVEL.

3'-1½" DIA. WHEELS.

SER 6 & 8 TON COVERED GOODS WAGON
S.R. DIAGRAM 1419.
NOTE: WHITE 'X' ON LEFT-HAND DOOR APPLIED TO VANS UNSUITABLE FOR
GUNPOWDER TRAFFIC DURING WORLD WAR ONE.

Above and left:

Figure 32 and Plate 85 These illustrations show the oldest and smallest SER covered goods wagon design to become SR property. Both depict diagram 1419 van No 5339 in a World War 1 lettering style. This was built in 1874 and was grounded at Tenterden Town (Kent & East Sussex Railway) some time after 1923. When photographed in August 1948, the 1914-18 lettering style was again visible — even including the white 'X' on the left-hand door, indicating that the van was not suitable for gunpowder traffic. It was allocated SR No 44688 — this and the post-Grouping lettering just being visible on the original print. *J. H. Aston*

Left:

Plate 86 A few of these vans became SR departmental stock. Here is van No 239S allocated to the London (East) Division engineer's electrification department, seen at London Bridge in November 1932. Built exactly 60 years earlier as SER No 5028, it was allocated SR running number 44676, but was transferred to engineer's use in May 1927 instead. The single timber brake block is on the far side. Final withdrawal occurred in November 1935, only two years before the last traffic department example was condemned. This was SR No 44721. *R. W. Kidner*

Above:

Plate 87 In 1877, production of the slightly longer vans to diagram 1421 commenced. Both these and diagram 1419 are characterised by the four vertical end uprights; however, the longer version has goods-type running gear and usually 3ft 1½ in or 3ft 2in-diameter Mansell wheels. East Kent Railway No 17 was photographed at Shepherdswell in the 1930s, by which time it had acquired spoke wheels, timber double-block brakes and replacement buffers. The bodywork has also had some extra strapping added, together with diagonal timber bracing to the doors, these latter alterations probably dating from late SECR ownership. The original SECR number and date of sale to the EKR are not recorded. *A. Riley Collection*

Below:

Figure 33 A drawing of diagram 1421 showing original condition. The last examples were withdrawn from traffic around 1933.

Selected Numbering Details for Diagrams 1419 and 1421

SR Diagram	SECR Nos	Survivors to SR Nos	Built By
1419	4004-30	44628-42, 44719/20	Brown Marshall 1863
1419	5007-36	44657-81, 44722	Ashford 1872
1419	5333-62	44682-705	Ashford 1874
1419	5550-69	44706-16	Ashford 1875-6
1421	5857-906	44990-5012	Ashford 1878
1421	6141-50	45013-17	Ashford 1877
1421	7075-124	45018-39	Ashbury Carriage & Iron Co 1880
			Recorded cost was £103 each.

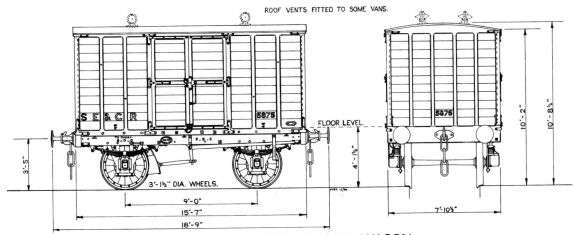

ROOF VENTS FITTED TO SOME VANS.

SER 8 TON COVERED GOODS WAGON

S.R. DIAGRAM 1421.

NOTE: SOME VEHICLES HAD A DIRECT-ACTING BRAKE LEVER.

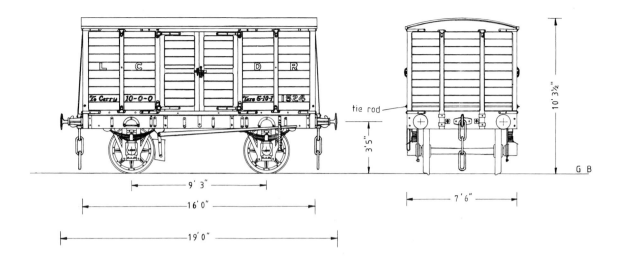

Above:
Figure 34 The LCDR covered goods wagon, as built from 1875 until 1892, although the majority were completed in the five years 1875-77, 1881/2. The drawing is based on that published in the *Railway Engineer* for June 1880, but it appears to be typical for all vans built under Kirtley's regime. They are easily distinguished from SER/SECR construction by the simpler body framing, with only one intermediate upright either side of the doors — SER designs had two. Brake gear was usually of the single-block variety, with a timber brake block. Some were later equipped with double-block gear, but it is doubtful if many acquired either-side brakes before final withdrawal. Although many were reconstructed by the SECR from 1912 onwards, only 46 survived to have Southern Railway numbers allocated and none remained in traffic department use beyond 1936. There was an earlier 15ft design, but only three remained in SECR traffic by 1919, SECR Nos being 9910, 9941/2.

According to the LCDR Appendix to the *Book of Rules and Regulations* to the *Working Timetable*, dated March 1898, there was just one van equipped with 3ft 7in-diameter Mansell wheels and Westinghouse pipes (LCDR No 1577, later SECR No 10225). This was probably the single van built in 1892, since there was a general arrangement drawing, No C2564, dated April 1892, described as a 'covered goods wagon for passenger trains'. Bodywork was identical to that shown above, but with passenger-type running gear and double-block brakes with a left-handed brake lever on one side only, screw couplings and long buffers. The document also states that the van was painted 'the same as horse boxes' — presumably passenger van brown to match the carriage stock livery of varnished teak. The vehicle was authorised to run in any passenger train except Boat or Granville Expresses.

The same Appendix also details LCDR van 1388 (SECR No 10036) as being suitable for running in 'SLOW but not in FAST Passenger Trains'. Perhaps this too was Westinghouse piped but retained its goods-type running gear? Livery in this instance is not recorded. Neither van survived to become Southern Railway stock. A view of a diagram 1423 vehicle in LCDR goods stock livery may be found in **Plate 7**.

Left:
Plate 88 An unidentified LCDR covered goods wagon, seen at Selsdon Road, on the joint line with the LBSCR, some time between 1903 and about 1912. The van is in original condition without any diagonal bracing to the doors or ends, and carries Wainwright period lettering, the wagon number just being visible at the right-hand end. The single-block brake gear is just visible on the far side. *Ian Allan Library*

Right:

Plate 89 LCDR covered goods No 1514 (later SECR No 10162), here running as SECR departmental number S40, at New Cross Gate in 1928. It was transferred to departmental stock in 1922, as a sponge cloth van for use between Ashford West and Margate, so just what it was doing in London is anybody's guess! Built in 1876 by S. J. Claye, it was reconstructed by the SECR in 1912 and was allocated SR departmental number 0735s, but was scrapped in September 1930, possibly without carrying its new number. Apart from the addition of diagonal bracing to the doors, the reconstruction seems to have made little difference to the appearance. *H. F. Wheeller*

Left:

Plate 90 Several LCDR van bodies were grounded as stores huts and the like. This is SECR No 10186 (ex-LCDR No 1538) photographed at Stoke Junction Halt on the Allhallows branch during the 1950s. World War 1 lettering is visible, including the 'not to be used for gunpowder' white 'X' on the top left-hand door panel. No Southern Railway number was allocated, so it is presumed that the van was grounded before 1923. *G. A. Hookham*

Right:

Plate 91 What was almost certainly the last LCDR goods vehicle to survive on its wheels could still be found at Abbey Wood in 1949. This diagram 1423 van was devoid of all identification and probably had not been capable of movement for many years. It remains substantially as built, save for the addition of diagonal door and end bracing. Demolition on site took place not long after the photograph was taken. *Lens of Sutton*

Left:

Plates 92, 93 and 94 All depict SR departmental number 611S at Stewarts Lane depot in 1936. This is one of the 10 original diagram 1422 vans of 1886, SER Nos 7600-9. In side elevation, they are almost identical to the previous SER design, but the flush-planked end was used for all subsequent SER/SECR vans until 1908. In this instance the end uprights are of timber, but most later vans used 'L' angles instead. This type of end construction gave an internal length of 15ft 2¼ in, and an external length of 15ft 5in, whereas the outside-framed style used on diagram 1421 gave corresponding dimensions of 15ft 0in and 15ft 7in respectively. Notwithstanding these changes, the SER included all 10 1886 vans on their diagram s1086, instead of the more accurate s1067 (which was not drawn until 1897). The Southern Railway at first included the vehicles on diagram 1421, but later amended this to 1422, although there were some minor differences between these and all later construction.

Van 611S entered departmental use in April 1932, its former numbers being SR 45046 and SECR 7608. Single-block brakes were originally provided on one side only, a second identical set being added in 1928. Passenger-type running gear with long buffers, springs and 3ft 6in-diameter Mansell wheels were provided from 1886. SECR No 1 oil axleboxes were used, but these were not the original 1886 fittings and probably date from 1914 onwards. The vehicle was withdrawn in October 1938. Van No 7604 (SR No 45042) is recorded as having full vacuum brakes, probably of the type drawn in **Figure 39** and remained so equipped until Southern Railway days. *All G. Hemingway*

Following completion of the 10 prototype vans of 1886, the wheelbase was then increased by 4in to 9ft 4in and 278 vans were then built to diagram 1420 between 1889 and 1900, whilst from 1898, 320 further diagram 1422 vehicles were completed, most of the latter being provided by outside contractors. These differed somewhat in underframe detail from the 1886 vehicles and are drawn in **Figure 35** on the next page. Numbering details are given below.

Clearly there was a greatly increased demand for covered goods wagons at this period. Interestingly, this increase in traffic was not matched by the LCDR, although financial constraints may have been to blame here.

Diagram 1422

SER/SECR Nos	Survivors to SR Nos	Built By	Brake Gear	Remarks
7600-9	45040-7	Ashford 1886	SB	Some later AVB.
8950-9049	45048-140	Ashbury 1898	ST	Goods-type running gear.
9100-49	45141-90	Ashbury 1899	ST	Goods-type running gear.
9150-299	45191-332	Oldbury 1899/1900	DB	Goods-type running gear.
Between 9907	45333-51	Ashford 1902	DB	20 replacements for
and 10270	and 45606*			LCDR stock.
	*10 tons capacity, all the rest were 8 tons			

SER Nos 8950-9049 were delivered painted dark red, possibly the passenger stock colour of crimson lake, with white lettering. Four became British Railway stock: Nos 45104, 45241 and 45343/8.

Right:
Plate 95 Diagram 1422 van No 9034, built by Ashbury Carriage & Iron Co in 1898, running as H. Pooley & Sons tool van 160S in 1935. The conversion dates from 1922 and involved the provision of oil lamps and skylights in the roof, end steps, side windows and full workshop facilities internally. SECR diagram s2522/2 was allocated and there were at least six such conversions: SR Nos 160S-2S and 221S-3S. Messrs Pooley & Sons held the contract for maintenance of SECR and SR weighing machines.
G. Hemingway

Left:
Plate 96 Another departmental conversion, No 424S was photographed at Ashford in June 1951, carrying ED red oxide livery. Built by the Oldbury Carriage & Wagon Co in October 1899, its SECR number was 9175. It became SR No 45216 at Grouping and was converted for departmental use in 1930. Double-block brake gear was originally fitted on one side only, a second set being added as part of the conversion. The end window was also added at the same time. *A. E. West*

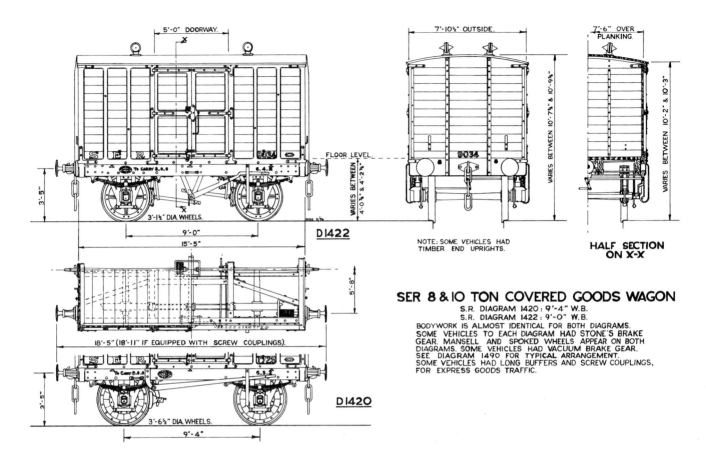

5'-0" DOORWAY.

S R 9034

FLOOR LEVEL

VARIES BETWEEN 4'-0¼" & 4'-2¾"

3'-5"

3'-1½" DIA. WHEELS.

9'-0"

15'-5"

D1422

7'-10½" OUTSIDE.

9034

VARIES BETWEEN 10'-7¾" & 10'-9¾"

NOTE: SOME VEHICLES HAD
TIMBER END UPRIGHTS.

7'-6" OVER
PLANKING.

VARIES BETWEEN 10'-2" & 10'-3"

HALF SECTION
ON X-X

5'-8"

18'-5" (18'-11" IF EQUIPPED WITH SCREW COUPLINGS).

S E R 1729

3'-5"

3'-6½" DIA. WHEELS.

9'-4"

D1420

SER 8 & 10 TON COVERED GOODS WAGON
S.R. DIAGRAM 1420: 9'-4" W.B.
S.R. DIAGRAM 1422: 9'-0" W.B.
BODYWORK IS ALMOST IDENTICAL FOR BOTH DIAGRAMS.
SOME VEHICLES TO EACH DIAGRAM HAD STONE'S BRAKE
GEAR. MANSELL AND SPOKED WHEELS APPEAR ON BOTH
DIAGRAMS. SOME VEHICLES HAD VACUUM BRAKE GEAR.
SEE DIAGRAM 1490 FOR TYPICAL ARRANGEMENT.
SOME VEHICLES HAD LONG BUFFERS AND SCREW COUPLINGS,
FOR EXPRESS GOODS TRAFFIC.

Above:
Figure 35 A combined drawing showing diagrams 1420 and 1422, as produced between 1889 and 1902. This depicts the majority of vehicles to both diagrams, although there were variations to brake and running gear amongst the 600 or so examples. J. Stone's either-side brake gear was favoured in the 1897-9 period; however, this employed a left-handed brake lever on one side and so failed to meet with Board of Trade approval after November 1911. Nevertheless, the railway companies were given such a long period to comply with these regulations that many SECR wagons were scrapped in the 1930s still carrying Stone's brake gear.

Left:
Plate 97 Diagram 1420 van 44756, carrying Southern Railway 1930s livery and lettering. This van was built at Ashford in June 1890, as SER No 1010, part of a batch of 70 equipped with long buffers, passenger-rated running gear and, originally, 3ft 6in-diameter Mansell wheels. No vacuum brakes or through vacuum pipe were provided, but double-block brakes were fitted on one side only. This van acquired a second set of brakes in September 1928 and had spoked wheels by the time it was photographed. Note that the increased buffer length was obtained in this instance by timber packings. The vehicle was scrapped in September 1935. *Edwards Bros*

Right:
Plate 98 Departmental van 116S at Stewarts Lane in 1935, built by Lancaster Carriage & Wagon Co in 1897, as SER No 8319. It became SR No 44979 until December 1929, when it was transferred to departmental service as a sponge cloth van. It is still in original condition complete with long buffers and Stone's either-side brake gear, with left-handed lever on the far side. The van was withdrawn in July 1938.
G. Hemingway

Left:
Plate 99 A vehicle from the same batch as 116S, showing the left-hand brake lever. SR No 44968 began life as SER No 8305 in June 1897 and ran until February 1938. From August 1931 until about 1935, the van was in internal use at various yards: Nine Elms, Southampton West, Millbrook and Wool. By 1936 it had returned to ordinary traffic, being photographed at Southampton Docks. *W. E. Boyd*

Right:
Plate 100 Diagram 1420 van No 44840, at Bricklayers Arms circa 1935. This was one of very few to retain its roof vents throughout. Built as SER No 1701 in 1895, it was equipped with goods-type running gear and short buffers, with single-block brakes on one side only. A second set of brakes was fitted in June 1928. From July 1937 it was stencilled 'To Work between Aylesford and Blackfriars only', probably for newspaper traffic and was withdrawn from this duty in September 1938.
G. Hemingway

Left:

Plate 101 An interesting comparison of liveries at Caterham in 1899. Diagram 1420 van No 1737 is in SER red livery, whilst brand-new diagram 1422 van No 919X behind is in SECR grey. Note that the van interior also appears to be grey. No 1737 was built in February 1896, one of 20 completed with full vacuum brakes and eight brake blocks, and cost £123. It later became SR No 44876, but had lost its vacuum brakes before 1923. An additional hand brake lever was provided in February 1932 and the van was withdrawn in August 1934. *R. C. Riley Collection*

Left:

Plate 102 A serious derailment to a goods train at Etchingham, on the Tonbridge-Hastings line, occurred on 27 October 1909. The cause was flooding occasioned by heavy rain. Underfloor details of a vacuum-fitted van are revealed — quite possibly one of the 1734-53 batch illustrated above. Details of the brake rodding and safety loops are visible. Further details may be found in **Figure 39** on page 88. *G. R. Stenner Collection*

Numbering Details of Diagram 1420 Vehicles

SER/SECR Nos	Survivors to SR Nos	Built By	Brake Gear	Remarks
429/39/52/61/3 72/96/9	44723-8	Ashford 1889/94	DB	Passenger-rated running gear; Nos 452/61 built in 1894.
605-27	44729-50	Ashford 1894	DB	Passenger-rated running gear.
1005-74	44751-817	Ashford 1890/1	DB	Passenger-rated running gear.
1646-62/96-1733	44818-72	Ashford 1895	SB	Goods-rated running gear.
1734-53	44873-90 and 45464*	Ashford 1896	AVB	Passenger-rated running gear and vacuum brakes.
1920/1	44891/2	Ashford 1900	ST	For Paramon's Ice traffic.
8230-329	44893-989	Lancaster C&W Co 1897	ST	Passenger-rated running gear.

*10 tons capacity, all the rest were 8 tons.
The last survivor in ordinary traffic was withdrawn in 1950.

Production of 15ft 5in-long covered goods wagons ceased in 1902. From 1904 until 1908 the design was lengthened to 16ft, resulting in diagram 1424. This probably indicates some LCDR influence, as its covered goods vehicles had been of this length since 1875, but this was still short by contemporary standards, many companies having already adopted 17ft, 18ft or longer. In total 110 vans were built and they were simply an enlarged version of the previous design.

Most had Hill's either-side brake gear, which remained acceptable to the Board of Trade as an either-side brake after November 1911. There were some limited experiments with door types, two vehicles being provided with pressed steel doors, whilst the last five built had three-part or LNWR pattern doors, ie drop flap at the bottom with cupboard-type doors over. These were probably SECR Nos 10104/73, 10220/40/53, later SR Nos 45421/39/50/2/4.

Above:

Plate 103 An excellent official broadside view of diagram 1424 van No 9944, bearing a repaint date of February 1909. The van was actually built new in December 1907, the reason for the photograph being the fitting of 'Lane' pressed-steel doors — one of two such vans so equipped, according to a paragraph in *The Railway Gazette* for 30 April 1909. Francis L. Lane was General Manager of The Leeds Forge Company and the firm had recently fitted these doors to some vehicles for export, so he had evidently convinced Wainwright to try them on the SECR. It is not known how long the two vans lasted with these fittings, but they remained the only ones so equipped. SECR No 9944 became SR No 45369 and ran until April 1938. The earliest vans had Stone's either-side brake gear, but most were provided with Hill's brake. *National Railway Museum*

Below:

Figure 36 Diagram 1424, showing details of Hill's brake gear.

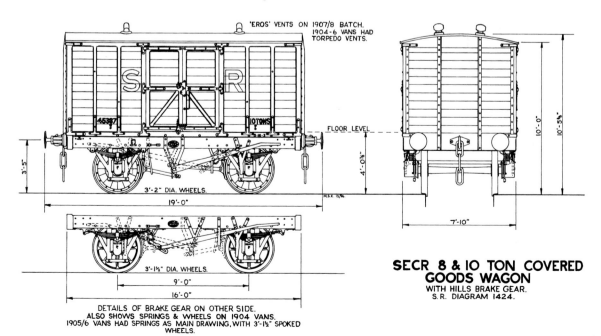

'EROS' VENTS ON 1907/8 BATCH.
1904-6 VANS HAD TORPEDO VENTS.

FLOOR LEVEL

3'-5"

3'-2" DIA. WHEELS.

19'-0"

3'-1½" DIA. WHEELS.

9'-0"

16'-0"

DETAILS OF BRAKE GEAR ON OTHER SIDE.
ALSO SHOWS SPRINGS & WHEELS ON 1904 VANS.
1905/6 VANS HAD SPRINGS AS MAIN DRAWING, WITH 3'-1½" SPOKED WHEELS.

4'-0½"

10'-0"

10'-5½"

7'-10"

SECR 8 & 10 TON COVERED GOODS WAGON
WITH HILLS BRAKE GEAR.
S.R. DIAGRAM 1424.

Above:
Plate 104 A rare view of a Wainwright-period wagon carrying British Railways lettering. No S45374 was photographed at Ashford as part of the 1948 series of official views. Built in March 1906 as SECR No 9960, the van was originally equipped with Hill's either-side brake gear, replaced by freighter brakes in May 1938. It was 'extensively repaired' in April 1939, which enabled it to survive to the BR period, one of only five vans to diagram 1424 to do so. Allocated to paper traffic between Aylesford and Blackfriars in July 1933, it survived until 1956. The other four BR survivors were Nos 45358/82 and 45427/55. *National Railway Museum*

Left:
Plate 105 Some diagram 1424 vans entered departmental use, such as No 1112S, seen at Eastleigh Works in September 1949. This started life as SECR No 10001 in 1907, becoming SR No 45387 and finally departmental 1112S in May 1937. Like No 45374 in **Plate 104** this van was also repaired considerably, receiving No 2 axleboxes in place of the original 'P' type. The Hill's brake gear was also replaced by freighter gear, probably at the same time.
D. Cullum

Diagram 1424
(SECR numbering of this diagram was somewhat random, so examples only are given.)

SECR Nos	SR Nos	Built By	Remarks
9929/64, 10003/5	45365/77/88/90	Ashford 1904	Passenger-type running gear, spoke wheels.
9934/90, 10110	45367/84, 45423	Ashford 1905/6	Goods-type running gear, spoke wheels.
1922-6, 10022	45358-62/97	Ashford 1907/8	Goods-type running gear, Mansell wheels.

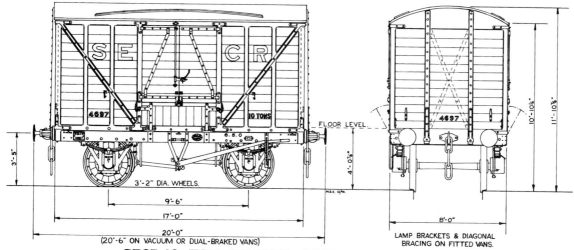

SECR 10 TON COVERED GOODS WAGON
S.R. DIAGRAM 1425.

NOTE: DRAWING DEPICTS UNFITTED VANS BUILT IN 1912.
1909 VEHICLES HAD 3'-1½" SPOKED WHEELS & HILLS BRAKE GEAR.
1911 VEHICLES HAD 3'-1½" SPOKED WHEELS, BUT WERE OTHERWISE AS 1912 VANS.
1914 VEHICLES HAD 3'-5" MANSELL WHEELS AND WERE VACUUM OR DUAL-BRAKED.
A FEW VANS FROM THE 1909/12 BATCHES WERE ALSO DUAL-BRAKED.
VACUUM & DUAL-BRAKED VANS HAD SECR TYPE 'C' AXLEBOXES.

Above:
Figure 37 The next development came in 1909, with diagram 1425. These wagons were 12in longer than the previous design and featured a much higher roof profile, with LNWR pattern three-part doors, but overall the design was still dated. The outside timber framing remained, with the addition of a diagonal brace, but the end construction also featured a return to outside timber framing. Ninety-eight were built, of which 19 were either vacuum or dual braked. All except one became SR stock at the Grouping.

Centre right:
Plate 106 Unfitted van No 4697, completed in February 1912. This has SECR 'P'-type axleboxes, Mansell wheels and freighter brake gear and was photographed at Ashford around 1924. Its SR number was 45471. The last survivor was SR No 45556, which ran until 1948. *G. P. Keen*

Below right:
Plate 107 A dual-fitted van from the same batch, SECR No 4691 was also completed in February 1912. This had Morton brake gear with one 18in vacuum cylinder and a Westinghouse brake cylinder. It originally had Mansell wheels, but retains its SECR 'C'-type axleboxes. This van became SR No 45465 and was transferred to departmental service in December 1943. Renumbered 1904S and allocated to the locomotive running department at Exmouth Junction shed, it was photographed there in September 1949. *Lens of Sutton*

Left:

Plate 108 Diagram 1425 van No 5001, built in December 1909, seen running as SR No 45476 at Bricklayers Arms in 1938. This was one of only two of the 50 1909 vehicles to be dual fitted. It has Morton brakes, spoke wheels and 'C'-type axleboxes. The livery is well worn, with chalked destinations 'Henfield' and 'Tovil' being legible. Note also the differing lengths of roof rainstrip on these vans: 1904S has a short one, that on 4697 is almost full length, whilst 45476 has one of intermediate length. Ribbed buffers are also fitted on van 45476. *G. Hemingway*

Left:

Plate 109 This picture shows the axlebox and brake gear, plus the 'SE&CR DUAL BRAKES' plate affixed to the solebar. The Westinghouse gear was removed from 1937 onwards and this van was one of the last survivors, being withdrawn in April 1945. By then only four others remained in general service. *G. Hemingway*

Diagram 1425
(Being charged to the renewals account, SECR numbering is somewhat random, therefore only a few examples are given below.)

SECR Nos	SR Nos	Date Built	Brake Gear	Fitted or Unfitted	Axle-Boxes	Type of Wheels	Remarks
4691-5	45465-9	2/12	M	Dual	'C'	Mansell	
4696-8	45470-2	2/12	F	Unfitted	'P'	Mansell	
4997-5006	45473-81	12/09	H	Unfitted	'P'	Spoke	No 5001 was dual fitted.
(4997 scrapped before 1923)							**(See Plates 108/9)**
9903/5/49	45483/4/90	7/09	H	Unfitted	'P'	Spoke	
9991,10006/23	45556-8	8/14	M	Vacuum	'C'	Mansell	No 9991 dual by 1922.
10048/68/72/90	45509/12/14/17	10/11	F	Unfitted	'P'	Spoke	
All were built at Ashford Works.							

The last of these vans were not completed until Maunsell was in charge, in fact just four days after the start of World War 1. At the time Maunsell was no doubt busy with more important matters than the construction of a small batch of dated vehicles, but he lost no time in having Lionel Lynes commence the design of a complete new range of wagons for future production. The first of these was the covered goods wagon. The only feature it had in common with diagram 1425 was the cupboard-door arrangement, no doubt requested by the Goods Manager. SECR No 10075 was the 'pattern' wagon and was completed in July 1915, but probably due to wartime conditions it was April 1918 before

any more could be built. In total 401 were completed, the last 100 by the Southern in 1925/6. Six were converted to ventilated vans early in 1923 and became SR diagram 1427; the rest were allocated to SR diagram 1426, irrespective of whether they had vacuum or hand brakes. Vacuum brake gear was fitted on 101 wagons, 50 of these being specifically allocated to Continental and Flushing meat traffic and lettered 'To Work between London, Folkestone and Dover Only'. Strictly speaking, diagram 1427 should fall within the ventilated covered goods wagon group, but because they began life as standard covered goods vehicles they are dealt with here.

Above:

Plate 110 The standard Maunsell-era covered goods wagon, to SR diagram 1426, was very different to what had gone before. SECR No 15757 was photographed when new in February 1919. It has a standardised steel underframe, SECR either-side (or lift-link) brake gear with two brake blocks, self-contained buffers and running gear to RCH standards. Livery is grey down to the undersides of the solebars, with black below. Attention is drawn to the worksplate, which reads 15767!! The painters have made an error, which hopefully was corrected before the vehicle entered traffic. No 15767 is correct for the wagon and it later became SR No 45784, surviving to the late 1950s. Being of more modern construction, almost all of these vans became BR stock and 35 remained in ordinary traffic when a census was taken in January 1961. By then many more were in departmental service and several of these passed to the preservation societies in the 1970s and 1980s. *SECR Official*

Left:

Plate 111 Diagram 1426 was a popular choice for departmental conversion from circa 1943 onwards. SR No 430S is seen at New Cross Gate in June 1947, being used as a sponge cloth van. Formerly SR No 47162, this is one of the batch completed by the Southern in 1925/6. The conversion took place in December 1946 and involved minimal work — no more than relettering and renumbering. Both pre and post-1936 lettering styles are visible. *Lens of Sutton*

Left:

Plate 112 A 1918-vintage diagram 1426 van, No S45682, is seen at Ashford Works in 1948. This was one of the vacuum-fitted examples, its SECR number being 15665. Morton brake gear is provided, with four brake blocks. The direct-acting brake lever is visible, the Morton clutch being on the other side. Livery is still SR brown, but with the 'S' prefix replacing the former company initials. This van was equipped with steam heating from March 1930 until 1931, possibly for banana traffic. It ran until 1955. *National Railway Museum*

Right:

Plate 113 The similarly vacuum-fitted van No 45683 (ex-SECR 15666) is seen in departmental use at Eastleigh in 1950, renumbered DS1921. The date of transfer to motive power department use was 1944. This shows the opposite side, with Morton clutch arrangement visible. *J. H. Aston*

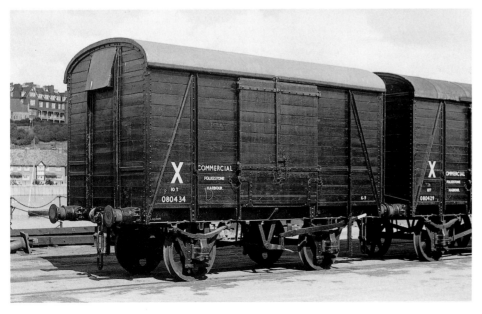

Left:

Plate 114 Two vans at Folkestone Harbour in September 1955, as internal user vehicles for the commercial department. Nos 080429 and 080434 sport smart black livery with white lettering. Their former running numbers are not known. *J. H. Aston*

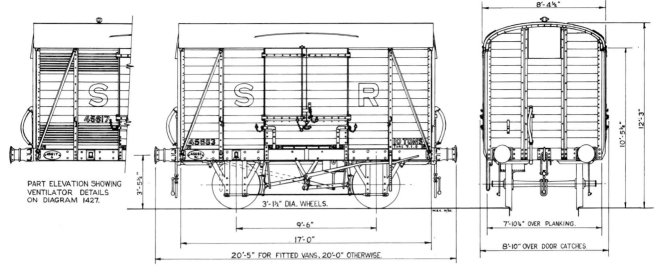

PART ELEVATION SHOWING VENTILATOR DETAILS ON DIAGRAM 1427.

3'-5½"

3'-1½" DIA. WHEELS.

9'-6"

17'-0"

20'-5" FOR FITTED VANS, 20'-0" OTHERWISE.

8'-4½"

12'-3"

10'-5½"

7'-10½" OVER PLANKING.

8'-10" OVER DOOR CATCHES

SECR 10 TON COVERED GOODS WAGON
S.R. DIAGRAMS 1426 & 1427.
FOR UNFITTED UNDERFRAME DETAILS REFER TO DIAGRAM 1355.

Above:
Figure 38 A combined drawing of diagrams 1426 and 1427.

Above:
Plate 115 Diagram 1427 ventilated van No S45618 (SECR 15601) at Ashford Works in September 1948. In 1923 six diagram 1426 vans were provided with side ventilators to make them suitable for fruit traffic. They were SECR Nos 15600-2/4-6, later SR Nos 45617-19/21-3. They were boarded to work between London, Folkestone and Dover only. These restrictions were rather belatedly removed during 1943/4. Built in 1918, this van lasted until 1955. Numbering details are as below. *National Railway Museum*

SECR Nos	SR Nos	Date Built	Brake Gear	Remarks
10075	45607	7/15	Probably M	Vacuum brakes
15591-690	45608-707	4/18-9/18	M	Vacuum brakes
15691-740	45708-57	11/18-2/19	M	Unfitted
15741-90	45758-807	2/19-4/19	LL	Unfitted
16091-190	45808-907	2/22-3/22	LL	Unfitted
None	47101-200	12/25-1/26	LL	Unfitted. SR order A26.
		All were built at Ashford Works.		

Ventilated Covered Goods Wagons

These were specifically for the conveyance of perishables such as meat, cheese, fish, fruit, flowers, etc, and also included some of the high-value perishables known as Grande Vitesse. This was carried at premium rates, much in excess of normal goods charges. Not all was of a perishable nature — the trade even included high French fashions from Paris! Whilst most was carried in passenger-rated vans, some goods vehicles were used. All had to be passenger-rated and have vacuum pipes at worst, or be fully-fitted at best.

The Continental goods depot for the SER was located within the low-level platforms at London Bridge but expansion of passenger traffic forced the construction of a new depot at Southwark Street, adjacent to Metropolitan Junction in 1901. This served until the opening of the British Railways Continental goods depot at Hither Green after Nationalisation. Most of the traffic originated at the Channel ports of Dover and Folkestone, but in SER days some came in via Queenborough pier. Prior to 1899 the LCDR had a small share in the traffic, so it also had some ventilated vans suitable for meat and fish traffic.

Four Southern Railway diagrams concern us in this group although, as already stated, the ventilated version of the Maunsell covered goods vehicle to diagram 1427, described on the previous page, could have equally been included in this section. Those conversions from cattle wagons to diagram 1489 are dealt with in Chapter 5.

SR Diagram	SECR Diagram	Origin	Capacity (tons)	Length Over Headstocks	Wheel-base	Known Period of Construction	Remarks
1489	s2514/1	SER	6	15ft 9in	9ft 4in	Rebuilt c1919	Ex-diagram 1512 cattle wagons.
1490	s1058	SER	8	16ft 0in	9ft 4in	1884	Originally unfitted, vac from c1904.
1491	s1095	LCDR	10	18ft 0in	10ft 0in	1876-1898	Goods and passenger-rated versions.
955*	Unknown	SER	8	21ft 0in	13ft 0in	1881	Grande Vitesse fruit vans.

*Passenger van series diagram number. These vans were classified as goods stock under SER/SECR ownership but were reclassified as passenger van stock by the Southern Railway.

Photographs of all these vehicles are conspicuous by their absence — perhaps many of the services on which they operated ran at night, resulting in fewer opportunities to record them. However, with only 34 examples extant in 1921 the lack of photographs is hardly surprising. A diagram 1489 conversion is just visible at Bricklayers Arms in the background of **Plate 188** on page 134, but the authors have yet to trace Diagram 1490 in any known photographs.

Below:
Figure 39 This drawing is based on the original general arrangement drawing of 1884. This shows a van with hand brakes only, but with large wheels, passenger-type running gear and long buffers and capable of running in the 'express' goods trains of the period. Vacuum provision, if any, was confined to a through pipe only. At some later date full vacuum brakes were provided. Only six vans were built, SER Nos 7424-9, later SR Nos 51227-32. The drawing shows a probable Southern Railway lettering style, although this is not confirmed by photographic evidence. SR livery should have been stone colour with Venetian red lettering but again, this has yet to be confirmed. The last van in traffic was withdrawn in 1938.

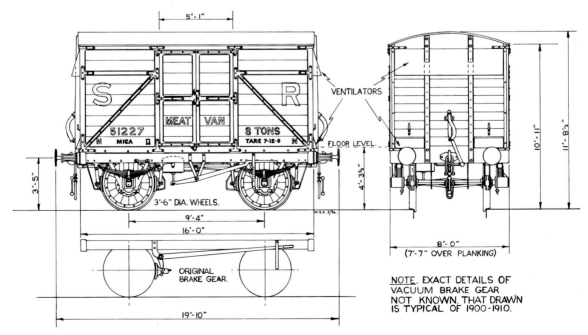

SER 8 TON MEAT VAN.   S.R. DIAGRAM 1490.

Right:
Plate 116 This goods train, headed by an unidentified '0' class 0-6-0 includes a diagram 1491 LCDR meat van as the first vehicle. This shows that such vans could appear singly in any goods train and were not confined purely to express services. The photograph dates from circa 1912 but yields little clue to the SECR lettering layout used on these vehicles. Goods-type running gear is provided, with a single-block brake. The second vehicle is a diagram 1558 goods brake van. *L. Ward*

Centre right:
Plate 117 Despite its poor quality, this shows an interesting variation of livery. LCDR meat van No 1001 (later SECR 11671) is seen carrying pre-1899 livery with the number surrounded by an oval panel. The significance of this marking is not known but it has not been recorded in any other known photograph. The van has goods-type running gear so the panel is not indicative of a passenger-rated vehicle. This van failed to become Southern Railway stock at the Grouping. *Authors' Collection*

Below:
Figure 40 The LCDR meat van showing passenger-rated running gear. For the goods-rated underframe the reader should refer to the diagram 1516 cattle wagon drawing on page 94.

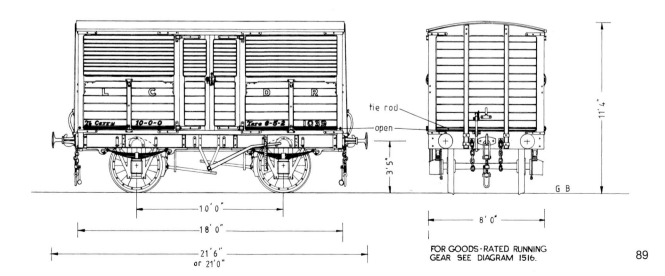

L C & D R   M E A T   W A G O N   SR DIAGRAM 1491

FOR GOODS-RATED RUNNING GEAR SEE DIAGRAM 1516.

Comparison of diagram 1491 and the cattle wagon to diagram 1516 will show that both types share a common bodywork design and that both came in passenger-rated and goods-rated versions. The former employed 3ft 7in-diameter Mansell wheels, the latter 3ft 0in spoke wheels. Westinghouse pipes were provided on the passenger-rated vehicles, although these had been stripped from all but four vans by the Grouping. The LCDR Appendix to the *Book of Rules and Regulations* dated March 1898 lists meat vans Nos 1029/38/9 (later SECR Nos 11699, 11708/9) as being passenger-rated and able to run in any train except boat or Granville expresses. These are noted as carrying passenger stock brown livery. SECR Nos 11708/9 eventually became SR Nos 51234/5 and both retained their Westinghouse pipes after 1923, whilst No 11699 is listed as being dual (ie both Westinghouse and vacuum) piped by 1923. This van was scrapped in that

year and was never allocated a Southern Railway number. LCDR Nos 1015/23/36/7, 2070/8/82 are also noted in 1898 as being suitable to run in 'SLOW but not in FAST passenger trains'. Presumably these had Westinghouse pipes but were otherwise goods-rated vans. SECR numbers of these were 11685/93, 11706/7, 11811/19/23 but only one (SECR 11707) survived to receive a Southern Railway number. As SR 51233 it was then stripped of Westinghouse pipes. SECR No 11811 also survived at the Grouping but was scrapped early in 1923. In contrast to No 11707 this van was dual piped. Alongside these, goods-rated vans 1040, 2066/9/74/80 (later SECR Nos 11710, 11807/10/15/21) all became SR stock as Nos 51236-40. It is not known if all were renumbered after 1923, nor whether they ever carried the SR insulated van livery of stone colour with Venetian red lettering. None was in traffic by 1935. All had been scrapped before 1935.

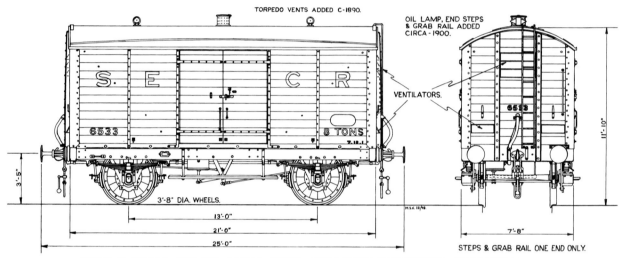

TORPEDO VENTS ADDED C-1890.

OIL LAMP, END STEPS & GRAB RAIL ADDED CIRCA - 1900.

VENTILATORS.

S. E C R

6533

8 TONS

7.18.1

6513

11'-10"

3'-5"

3'-8" DIA. WHEELS.

13'-0"

21'-0"

25'-0"

7'-8"

STEPS & GRAB RAIL ONE END ONLY.

M.S.K. 12/98.

SER 8 TON FRUIT VAN FOR GRANDE VITESSE TRAFFIC
S.R. DIAGRAM 955 - PASSENGER-RATED STOCK AFTER 1923.

Above:
Figure 41 The last vehicle to be dealt with in this section is the Grande Vitesse fruit van to diagram 955. This was totally unlike any other SER vehicle, being inside-framed and flush-planked: altogether a remarkably modern-looking van for 1881. These vans closely resemble the LBSCR Grande Vitesse van illustrated in **Plate 5** of Volume 2 and this similarity may be more than coincidental as both served the same class of traffic. The drawing shows the vans in their final form with roof vents, oil lamps and access ladders at one end. It also shows a typical Maunsell-period lettering style.

Right:
Plate 118 A Grande Vitesse van at Faversham around 1904. No details of lettering are visible but it is thought likely that the vans were painted in the passenger stock livery of crimson lake, later altered to dark brown during World War 1. After 1923 they were definitely painted in SR passenger stock green livery. SER numbers were 6533-44, in the goods stock series. Southern Railway passenger stock numbers were 1870-81. They were withdrawn between 1929 and 1935, the last survivor being SR No 1876. *Dr Evers, courtesy R. L. Ratcliffe*

Chapter 5.
Livestock Vehicles

The SECR owned around 350 vehicles suitable for the conveyance of livestock at the Grouping, comprising six basic designs with several minor variations — a little under 3% of the total wagon stock. However, as the photograph below demonstrates, much of the cattle traffic was carried in other companies' stock and this situation had probably not altered since pre-Grouping days — any livestock traffic originating outside the SECR area being delivered in the originating companies' vehicles. The SER had some vehicles specifically for sheep traffic, but the last of these was withdrawn during World War 1. As with most railways, the earliest SER cattle trucks were open vehicles and amazingly one of these survived on the Kent & East Sussex Railway into the 1930s.

Above:
Plate 119 A Bricklayers Arms to Ashford cattle special passing Pluckley in August 1933 headed by 'O1' class 0-6-0 No A439. The train consists of, maybe, 40 wagons from all the Big Four companies. Ashford had, until recently, a large cattle market situated midway between the Chatham and South Eastern stations and this was served for many years by its own siding. When one thinks of cattle wagons one normally associates them, naturally enough, with cattle, but in Kent the traffic carried in them was very often sheep raised on the extensive marsh levels. *Lens of Sutton*

With a few exceptions, SECR cattle wagons were equipped with vacuum pipes; some also had Westinghouse pipes in addition, so most were able to run in express goods and in passenger trains. The special cattle vans (pedigree cattle vans in SECR parlance) were used for the conveyance of prize stock and the like and were mostly either dual piped or vacuum braked with through Westinghouse pipes. These have not been dealt with separately as three of the four designs had a very similar goods-rated counterpart and in SECR days all were numbered within the goods wagon series. In several instances the passenger vans were subsequent conversions from goods-rated stock and, to complicate matters further, several of them were employed as goods stock in the late SECR and early Southern Railway period, without modification, simply to ease a temporary shortage of vehicles.

After 1923 the pedigree vehicles became passenger van stock and were renumbered and repainted accordingly in green livery. A handful of the Maunsell/Lynes vans survived until 1951 but it is doubtful if any received the British Railways livery of crimson lake.

By 1923 the goods cattle wagons were, with one exception, large vehicles, ie, for the purpose of charging, 18ft or more in length. One medium design from the SER still survived and at least seven of these had been rebuilt as meat vans circa 1919. They are mentioned briefly in Chapter 4 (page 88) but are described here. The majority of the Wainwright period vehicles were withdrawn by 1940, but the Maunsell/Lynes design of 1917 was adopted as an early Southern Railway standard with 350 more being completed between 1923 and 1928. A few of these survived until 1966.

Details of the Southern Railway diagrams are given below, in approximate chronological order. Diagram numbers 1049-52 were the passenger-rated vehicles.

SR Diagram	SECR Diagram	Origin	Capacity (tons)	Length Over Headstocks	Wheel-base	Known Period of Construction	Remarks
1512	s1040	SER	6 and 8	15ft 9in	9ft 4in	1866-84	Seven rebuilt as meat vans circa 1919, to diagram 1489.
1516	s1090	LCDR	10	18ft 0in	10ft 0in	1873-98 (1892-passenger)	Both passenger and goods-rated versions.
1514	s1039	SER	8, 9 and 10	18ft 3in	10ft 6in	1888-1900	Very similar to diagram 1513.
1049	s1049	SER	7 and 8	18ft 3in	10ft 6in	1891 and 1893	Passenger version of diagram 1514.
1513	s1039	SER	8 and 10	18ft 6in	10ft 6in	1895-1907	Very similar to diagram 1514.
1050	s1049	SECR	8	18ft 6in	10ft 6in	1907	Passenger version of diagram 1513.
1052	s1042	SECR	7 and 8	20ft 0in	10ft 6in	1904/8/11	With stockman's compartment.
1517	s1075	SECR	10	19ft 0in	10ft 6in	1908	Very similar to diagram 1518.
1518	s1047	SECR	10	19ft 0in	10ft 6in	1912 (Bristol W&C Co)	Very similar to diagram 1517 with RCH wheels.
1515	s2139/7	SECR	10	19ft 0in	10ft 6in	One in 1917, rest 1921-8	Most built by SR. Some later to diagram 1051.
1051	None	SECR	7 and 8	19ft 0in	10ft 6in	Ex-diagram 1515 in 1922	Passenger version of diagram 1515.

As will be noted from the table, there were a number of similarities between the 11 diagrams and in reality there were only six basic designs. The SER grouped all its large cattle wagons on to two diagrams — one for the goods version and one for passenger — ignoring the fact that there was a 3in discrepancy in length between the 1888 and 1895 designs. In service this was of little consequence; all that concerned the traffic department was their passenger or goods status. The Southern Railway attempted to sort the wagons out but actually failed to allocate a diagram number to three vehicles built in 1888. These were part of a batch of six, SER numbers being 7839-44. Their details remain blank in the SR Registers, save for withdrawal dates between 1924 and 1927. It is therefore uncertain if they were different to any of the diagrams above. However, it is most likely that they were the prototype 18ft 3in vehicles to diagram 1514 and are listed accordingly.

Left:
Plate 120 Taken at Redhill between 1900 and 1908, this view shows SER medium cattle wagon No 5679, one of a batch of 60 built in 1876/7. This particular vehicle was condemned in 1908 and just five of the batch survived to become SR stock as diagram 1512 at the Grouping. The seven meat van conversions to diagram 1489 also came from this batch. SECR numbers of these were 5697-9, 5701/2/5/6. All except No 5701 became SR stock and were then allocated numbers 51221-6. The conversion simply involved the infilling of the open sections of the sides with louvres, provision of roof ventilators and addition of through vacuum pipes. Internally, meat hooks were incorporated and what may be a set of these is visible loaded into an LCDR open goods wagon in **Plate 14**. **Figure 42** on the next page gives details of both versions. Also seen at Redhill is what may be a sheep truck of circa 1852 vintage, from the number series SER 1754-83. The last of these was withdrawn around 1916.
E. Pouteau, courtesy G. R. Stenner

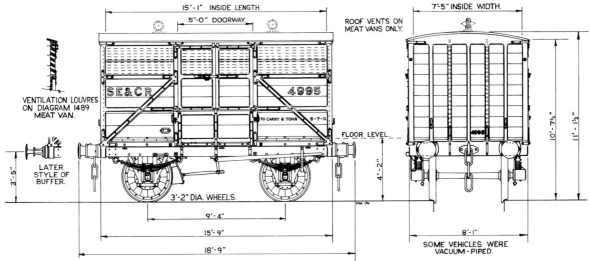

SER 6 & 8 TON MEDIUM CATTLE WAGON & MEAT VAN
S.R. DIAGRAMS 1512 & 1489.

Above:
Figure 42 This figure shows the only medium-sized cattle wagon inherited from the SECR at the Grouping. Just 17 survived at this date and few were renumbered or repainted in SR livery. The last survivor was withdrawn in 1934.

Left:
Plate 121 One of these wagons in SER livery — the wagon number was displayed in the same position as the company initials, but at the right-hand end. This shows the most obvious feature of these vehicles, namely the four intermediate end uprights — a detail they share with contemporary covered goods wagons to diagrams 1419 and 1421. This example was vacuum piped, but most had hand brakes only. *G. R. Stenner Collection*

Below:
Plate 122 Diagram 1512 cattle wagon No 4989 at Ashford in 1924, showing a variation in lettering style. This wagon was built in 1872 and was allocated SR No 52522. To the right is a similar wagon carrying larger lettering. It also has more modern buffers and spring shackles so may be from the same batch as that illustrated in **Plate 120**. To the left is diagram 1518 wagon No 14089 which is featured in **Plate 131**. Note the liberal application of limewash used to disinfect the vehicles at this period. *G. P. Keen*

L C & D R CATTLE WAGON   S R DIAGRAM 1516

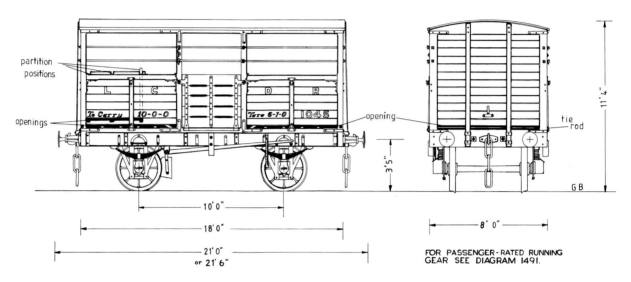

Above:

Figure 43 The LCDR cattle wagon design, later allocated SR diagram 1516. Six remained in stock in January 1923 but this total had reduced to just two by the time the renumbering scheme was worked out later in the year. The bodywork was the same as the meat van to diagram 1491, but with a drop-flap door and open section of upper bodywork in place of louvres. Like the meat vans, there were both goods and passenger-rated versions, the former dating from 1873, the latter from 1892. Goods-rated running gear is shown above and details of the passenger-rated version may be found on the meat van drawing on page 89.

The LCDR Appendix to the *Book of Rules and Regulations* to the *Working Timetables* for March 1898 gives some details of the vehicles. This lists wagon numbers 1013/16/20/31/4/44/64 (later SECR Nos 11683/6/90, 11701/4/14/34) as being passenger-rated with Westinghouse pipes, painted in passenger stock brown livery and being capable of running in any train except boat or Granville expresses, whilst numbers 1009/17 (later SECR Nos 11679/87) could run in 'SLOW but not in FAST passenger trains'. As with the covered goods and meat vans in this same category, we presume that these two were goods-rated but had the benefit of through Westinghouse pipes. None of the wagons listed survived to the Grouping. Both wagons which had Southern Railway numbers allocated (LCDR Nos 1019/45, later SECR Nos 11689 and 11715) were goods-rated and were devoid of Westinghouse pipes. Neither would have survived long in SR ownership.

No suitable photographs of LCDR cattle wagons have yet been found, so we have made use of an almost identical Hull & Barnsley Railway wagon which is reproduced **opposite**. The lettering style depicted in **Figure 43** is based on photographic evidence of a part view taken at Longhedge in the 1890s.

Another part view in the author's collection, taken circa 1898 at Herne Hill, appears to show Westinghouse-piped vehicle No 1064. This has the wagon number on the bottom plank (ie one plank lower than shown above), but has the words

To Be Returned At Once EMPTY
To HERNE HILL Sorting Sidings

in two lines of small lettering above the wagon number. Perhaps all the LCDR's Westinghouse-piped wagons were so lettered?

Left:

Plate 123 William Kirtley, in his capacity as Consulting Mechanical Engineer to the Hull, Barnsley & West Riding Junction Railway & Dock Co, provided some almost identical cattle wagons between 1883 and 1885. No 490 was a goods-rated example. This company must take the honours for the most initials displayed on a goods wagon! A photograph also exists of passenger-rated wagon No 4101 but this is more simply lettered 'H&BR'. *Authors' Collection*

Right:

Plate 124 What appear to be three examples to SR diagram 1513, about to be loaded with military horses, are illustrated here at Maidstone Barracks circa 1899. The two SER large cattle wagon designs are very similar and difficult to distinguish in photographs so we may also be looking at examples to diagram 1514 as well. Military horses were a regular load for cattle wagons at that time, only the officers' horses would travel in horseboxes. Note that the wagon in the centre sits slightly higher on its springs — maybe indicative of a different diagram. *Authors' Collection*

Left:

Plate 125 Military traffic again but this time on the LSWR, at Okehampton, Devon. Diagram 1514 cattle wagon No 1942 is visible, one of a batch of 12 completed in 1899/1900. This was later allocated SR No 52567, but failed to survive beyond 1933. On the right is a special cattle van to either diagram 1049 or 1050, in passenger van stock livery with what appears to be unshaded gold or yellow lettering. The italics over the company initials read 'To be returned to Tonbridge Station'. A left-handed brake lever is visible, suggesting that the van is equipped with Stone's brake gear. *J. Tatchell Collection*

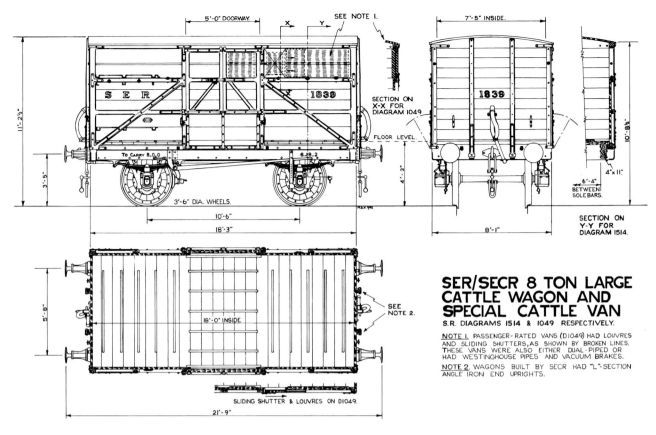

SER/SECR 8 TON LARGE CATTLE WAGON AND SPECIAL CATTLE VAN
S.R. DIAGRAMS 1514 & 1049 RESPECTIVELY.

NOTE I. PASSENGER-RATED VANS (D1049) HAD LOUVRES AND SLIDING SHUTTERS, AS SHOWN BY BROKEN LINES. THESE VANS WERE ALSO EITHER DUAL-PIPED OR HAD WESTINGHOUSE PIPES AND VACUUM BRAKES.
NOTE 2. WAGONS BUILT BY SECR HAD "L"-SECTION ANGLE IRON END UPRIGHTS.

Above and below:

Figures 44 and 45 The 1888 design, with an overall length of 18ft 3in, is shown *above* in **Figure 44** whilst *below* is **Figure 45**, which shows the very similar 1895 design, some 3in longer. Without a running number being visible it is often difficult to tell the two diagrams apart. Both types had an equivalent pedigree cattle van, with louvres and sliding shutters in place of the open upper portion of bodywork. The different types of drop-flap door may be a useful identification point but even this is not guaranteed to go with any one diagram. The 1895 design was finally the more numerous with at least 84 wagons; the 1888 vehicles never exceeded 40 examples. Withdrawal commenced before 1923 by which date the totals had been reduced to 73 and 25 respectively. As more modern wagons were built, the totals fell still further until the last wagons were deleted in 1938 (diagram 1514 No 52542) and 1940 (diagram 1513 No 52540). The special cattle vans fared no better, the last survivor being diagram 1050 van No 3738, condemned in 1935. Indeed, all examples to diagram 1049 were scrapped prior to 1932 and only Nos 3731/2/44/5 ever carried SR livery.

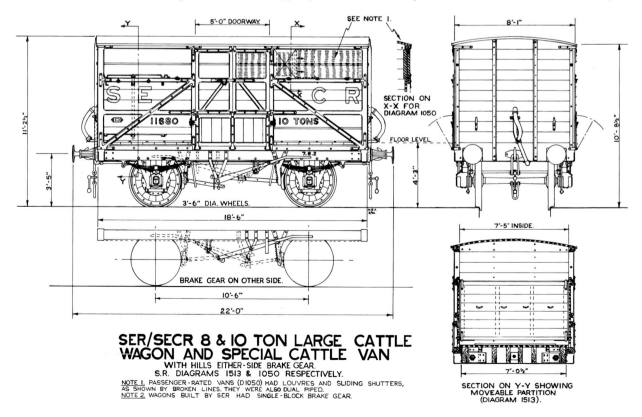

SER/SECR 8 & 10 TON LARGE CATTLE WAGON AND SPECIAL CATTLE VAN
WITH HILLS EITHER-SIDE BRAKE GEAR.
S.R. DIAGRAMS 1513 & 1050 RESPECTIVELY.

NOTE I. PASSENGER-RATED VANS (D1050) HAD LOUVRES AND SLIDING SHUTTERS, AS SHOWN BY BROKEN LINES. THEY WERE ALSO DUAL PIPED.
NOTE 2. WAGONS BUILT BY SER HAD SINGLE-BLOCK BRAKE GEAR.

SECTION ON Y-Y SHOWING MOVEABLE PARTITION (DIAGRAM 1513).

Above left and right:

Plates 126 and 127 The last SER large cattle wagon to run in main line service may have been withdrawn in 1940, but this was not the last one in existence. SECR No 1944 was sold to the Kent & East Sussex Railway in 1928 and survived in virtual disuse as their No 13 until Nationalisation. The end view was taken at Rolvenden circa 1939, when traces of faded SECR livery, including the numbers, were still visible. The side view shows the wagon awaiting breaking up at Headcorn in 1948. The allocated SR number was 52569 but this was never carried. The wagon dates from December 1898 and its recorded original cost was £120. *Both SR Official photographs*

Numbering details of SER/SECR 18ft cattle wagons

(Numbers include those for diagram 1052, described on the next page. SECR and SR numbering of the cattle wagons was somewhat muddled, as will be seen.)

SR Diagram	SECR Nos	Survivors to SR Nos	Date Built	Brake Gear	Remarks
1514?	7839-44	52576/7, 52612	1888	SB	No diagram in SR register.
1050	1806-11	3738-43	1907	H	Dual piped.
1513	1812-24	52578-88/32/89	1906/7	H	
1513	1825-37	52533-41	1902	Poss ST}	Replacements for ex-
1513	11698, 11703/13, 11717/37/53/63	52570-2	1902	Poss ST}	SER and LCDR stock.
1513	1850-71	52550-61	1895/96	SB	
1513	11680, 11723/82/3, 11806/16	52590-5	1906	H	Replacements for ex-LCDR stock.
1513	13121-37	52596-611	1904	H	
1514	1280/81/6/7	3733 only (as prize cattle van)	1891*	SB	Number 1281 later to diagram 1049.
1049	1278/9/82-5	3731/2/4-7	1891*	SB	Vacuum brake with Westing-house pipe.
1514	1838-43/6-9	52542-9	1893*	SB	
1049	1844/5	3744/5	1893*	SB	Dual piped.
1514	1935-46	52562-9	1899/1900	SB	
1052	95-100	3758-63	1908	H}	With stockman's com-
1052	11671/3/8	3764-6	1911	H}	partment and all were
1052	13138-40	3767-9	1904	H}	dual piped.

*It is not entirely clear which of the 1891/3 vehicles were built as pedigree vans or ordinary stock.
All were built at Ashford Works. Nos 3731-69 were SR passenger van series numbers.

Left:

Plate 128 Four cattle wagons stand at the head of a down goods train at Orpington, circa 1927, all freshly repainted in SR livery. The leading vehicle is diagram 1513 wagon No 52552 (ex-SECR No 1856). This ran from 1895 until 1933. Next come examples to diagrams 1518 and 1515, followed by one of LBSCR origin. All are loaded with fruit baskets — a useful return load which saved an otherwise empty journey back to country stations. In later years petrol in 'jerry cans' was another load considered suitable for cattle trucks.
Lens of Sutton

Right:

Plate 129 Twelve 'Improved cattle wagons with stockman's compartment' were completed in three separate batches between 1904 and 1911. SECR No 98 (later SR No 3761) was photographed at Ashford circa 1924, carrying what is presumed to be passenger stock livery. This is one of the 1908 vehicles and it ran until April 1937. Note the 'Return to Redhill when empty' instruction. Three each were allocated to Redhill, Tonbridge, Ashford and Faversham. To the left, 1904-built van No 13140 may just be seen, whilst to the right is an ex-LBSCR special cattle van. *G. P. Keen*

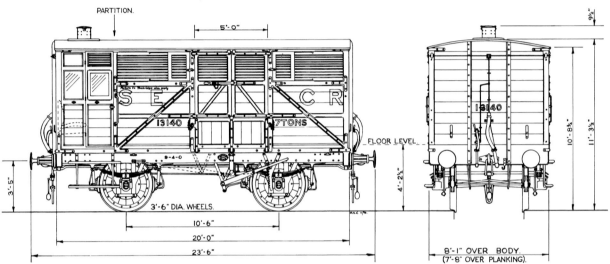

SECR 7 TON IMPROVED CATTLE WAGON WITH STOCKMANS COMPARTMENT.
S.R. DIAGRAM 1052.
1904 DESIGN AS DRAWN, 1908/11 VEHICLES DIFFER IN DETAIL.

Above:

Figure 46 Details of diagram 1052 and showing the opposite side to the photograph. There were slight differences between the three batches, such as the length of the springs. End steps do not seem to have been provided.

Right:

Plate 130 From 1908 the goods cattle wagon design was updated slightly, with an increased overall length of 19ft 0in. Two designs were produced with essentially the same bodywork: diagram 1517 with 3ft 6in-diameter Mansell wheels and diagram 1518 with 3ft 1½in-diameter RCH wheels. The former numbered just 15 examples, the latter 100 wagons. Diagram 1517 wagons were built at Ashford, the rest being supplied by Bristol Wagon & Carriage Co. This is SECR No 14074 (later SR No 52752) when new in September 1912. The contract specified that the lettering and numbers were to be in 7in-high characters. *The Science Museum*

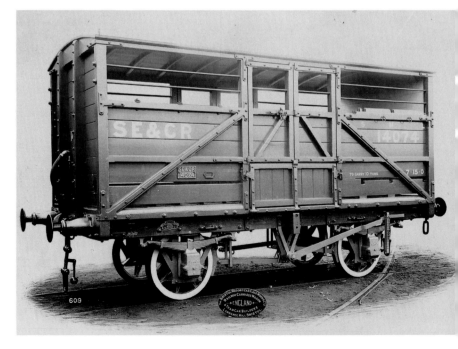

Right:

Plate 131 Diagram 1518 wagon No 14089 at Ashford, circa 1924, in the company of diagram 1512 wagon No 4989 to the right (seen in **Plate 122**), and an unidentified diagram 1513 or 1514 vehicle to the left. All are well stained with limewash. In later years either a chemical cleaner or plain water was used, since by 1930 there are usually no signs of the white staining. Wagon No 14089 later became SR No 52767 and lasted until the late 1940s. Freighter brake gear was standard on this diagram, as were through vacuum pipes. *G. P. Keen*

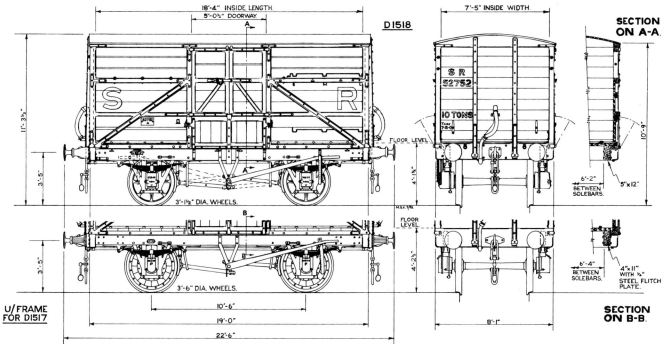

SECR 10 TON LARGE CATTLE WAGON 1908 & 1912 DESIGNS.
S.R. DIAGRAMS 1517 (1908 DESIGN) & 1518 (1912 DESIGN).

Above:

Figure 47 This figure gives details of both the Wainwright 19ft cattle wagons. As yet the authors have not traced a good photograph of a wagon to diagram 1517, the above information being provided using a general arrangement drawing. Below are numbering details of these and the Maunsell/Lynes wagon designs featured on the next three pages.

SR Diagram	SECR Nos	SR Nos	Date Built	Remarks
1517	11695/7, 11702/21/7/54/ 60/1/4/7/72/4/6/92, 11800	52654-68	Ashford 1908	Hill's brake gear on one side only. Most scrapped 1929-40.
1518	13991-14090	52669-768	Bristol 1912	Freighter brakes and RCH wheels.
1515	11670, 12071-100, 12501-20	52613-51	One Ashford 1917, rest 1921	12 converted to pedigree vans in 1922.
1051	12074/7/8/80/8/90/ 3/4/6/7/9, 12512	3746-57	Converted at Ashford 1922	Passenger version of diagram 1515.

In addition, further examples to diagram 1515 were completed by the Southern Railway between 1923 and 1928, these being numbered 52769-881 and 53391-627 (SR order Nos A25, A106 and A165). Also, goods-rated wagon No 12510, completed in 1921, was converted into an additional passenger-rated van at Ashford in March 1925, taking the SR number 3770. Numbers 3747-9/51/2/5/70 survived to British Railways ownership.

Above:

Plate 132 An excellent official broadside of the Maunsell/Lynes 'pattern' (ie prototype) cattle wagon to SR diagram 1515, bearing a paint date of 12 December 1917. No further examples were constructed until March 1921. Clearly visible are the SECR No 2 axleboxes and the Morton brake gear with which most of these wagons were equipped. Only the special cattle wagon conversions seem to have been provided with the SECR either-side or lift-link brake. The letters 'S', 'M' and 'L' refer to the position of the interior partition — small, medium or large — for the purpose of charging. It was SECR practice to place the wagon lettering on the side sheeting, where it was often obliterated by limewash. After 1923 the Southern put most of the lettering on the ends, which solved this particular problem. SECR No 12071 became SR No 52614 and remained in service until May 1948. *SECR Official*

Right:
Plate 133 Diagram 1515 wagon No 53589, one of those completed by the Southern in 1928, is seen far from home at Renfrew, Scottish Region, in August 1946, still carrying pre-1936 SR lettering. *A. G. Ellis*

Right:
Plate 134 The same wagon as out-shopped at Ashford in October 1948, still carrying SR brown livery but with the 'S' prefix to the number in place of the letters 'SR'. This wagon ran until 1954. *National Railway Museum*

Below:
Figure 48 The Maunsell/Lynes cattle wagon design. The inverted vee framing on the ends was a most unusual and distinctive feature.

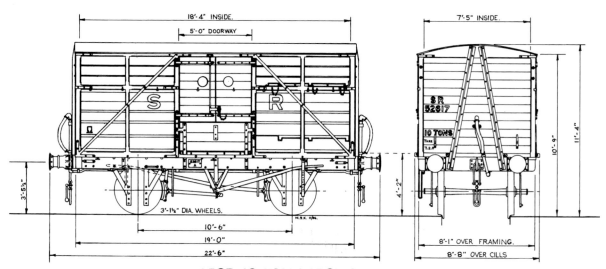

SECR 10 TON LARGE CATTLE WAGON
S.R. DIAGRAM 1515.
FOR PASSENGER-RATED VERSION SEE DIAGRAM 1051.

101

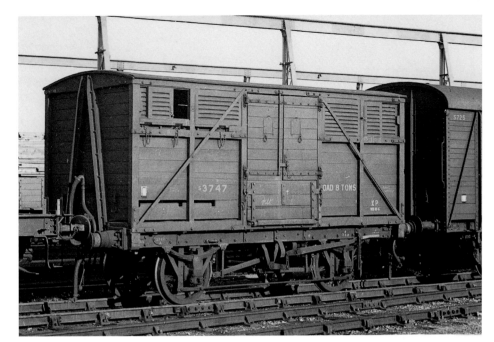

Left:

Plate 135 The special cattle van equivalent of diagram 1515, converted just prior to the Grouping. No S3747 is seen at Eastleigh Carriage Works awaiting scrapping in September 1949. Built as a goods-rated vehicle in 1921, SECR No 12074, it was modified less than a year later into the form shown. The livery is SR passenger stock green with black ends, but whether the green is Maunsell or Bulleid shade cannot be stated. Lettering is yellow for the number and load inscription, but the 'XP' and 'WB 10ft 6in' are in white. These special cattle vans were originally dual piped but this was later altered to full vacuum brakes, together with through steam heating pipes. This allowed the vans to run in any passenger train. The last survivor was SR No 3752, withdrawn in July 1951. *J. H. Aston*

Below:
Figure 49 The Maunsell/Lynes special cattle van. This shows SR post-1936 lettering.

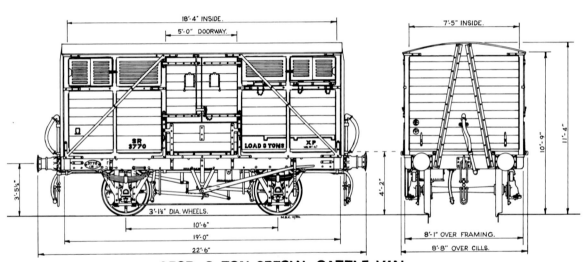

SECR 8 TON SPECIAL CATTLE VAN
S.R. DIAGRAM 1051.

Left:

Plate 136 For our final illustration in this chapter we return to the seasonal problem of sheep transportation. This matter exercised the minds of the drawing office staff at Ashford from time to time between 1917 and 1921, several designs being prepared of which only this one seems to have been acted upon. In August 1917 drawing No 4886 was issued for a 12-ton convertible open goods or sheep wagon. One hundred such vehicles were ordered in the following year, the end result being No 12121, seen as out-shopped in March 1919. It appears to have been the only one completed and may never have run in traffic in the form illustrated, as No 12121 is recorded as being booked out of Ashford Works in September 1919 as a standard seven-plank open wagon, later becoming SR diagram 1355 vehicle No 15598. As such it lasted until June 1946. In all probability, the Board of Trade failed to approve the design. *SECR Official*

Chapter 6.
Goods Brake Vans

Some 300 goods brake vans were passed to the Southern Railway from the SECR, ranging from an ancient incline brake of 1865 vintage through to modern 25-tonners, as up-to-date as any in the country. The majority, however, were small outside-framed timber vehicles with a tare weight of not more than 10 tons, already outclassed even by the standards of 1923. Despite this, some were as little as 20 years old at the Grouping and, surprisingly, a few were to remain in use for another 20 years. At the other extreme the Maunsell/Lynes design of 1918 went on to become a Southern Railway standard until 1928, after which the underframe remained in production for almost all subsequent SR goods brake vans built down to 1948, albeit with redesigned details.

The LCDR contribution did not in fact reach the Southern as a goods brake — the authors have so far traced just two remaining in departmental service at the Grouping. One was a stores van, the other very much altered as a match truck for a goods department crane. Both the LCDR and the SER designs had much in common with their contemporary covered goods vehicles, but in 1898 the South Eastern completed the first of its 'Midland Railway style' 20-ton vans. These were a carbon-copy of the standard MR six-wheeled van to that company's diagram 393, which had been built since 1886. Exactly how the South Eastern came to use a Midland Railway design is not known to the authors, but it was probably the result of an inter-working agreement between the two companies. There were several locations at which traffic was passed from one system to the other, in particular via the Metropolitan Widened lines across London and there were probably locations where there might not have been clearance for the outward opening doors of SER brake vans to open far enough to allow the guard to leave the van. This could be a serious problem and was one which did not exist with the MR design. In time, the SECR modified the design somewhat, resulting in a purely South Eastern vehicle.

In terms of livery, the LCDR did not see fit to alter its standard specification of grey overall. However, on the SER things were different. The usual livery of light red was replaced by dark reddish-brown sides with bright red ends, black ironwork with white lettering shaded in black. The black ironwork seemed to vary in its application — for some vans this was confined just to buffer rods and below solebars, but in other cases all body ironwork was picked out in black. Regrettably, these colours do not reproduce well in the monochromatic photographs of the period. The best reproduction of the livery appears in **Plate 8** on page 15. After 1899 the SECR appears to have standardised on grey overall for the entire wagon fleet, with no mention of bright red ends for brake vans. This is confirmed by a specification dated 1900 and also by an Edwards Bros drawing published in 1920 of the prototype Maunsell/Lynes 25-ton brake van. The latter gives the colour as dark lead bodywork, black below solebars with a white roof and lettering. There is no mention of red ends, despite the livery adopted by several of the preservation societies for these vehicles.

SECR/SR Diagrams Allocated to the Brake Vans, in Approximate Chronological Order

SR Diagram	SECR Diagram	Origin	Tare (tons)	Length Over Headstocks	Wheel-base	Known Period of Construction	Remarks
1556	Unknown	SER	12	13ft 6in	8ft 3in	1865/70/3	Folkestone Harbour incline brake vans.
—	s1089	LCDR	8 and 10	18ft 0in	9ft 6in	1874-99	'Road' vans.
—	Possibly s1063	SER	6	No details in SR registers	No details in SR registers	1872-8	Withdrawn in 1924. Not renumbered.
1552	s1064	SER	9 and 10	16ft 0in	9ft 0in	1885-93	With lookouts. Vacuum fitted or piped
1553	s1063 and s1065	SER	10	16ft 0in	9ft 0in	1879-1903	'Road' vans. Several variations in design.
1554	s1063 and s1065	SER	10 each	16ft 0in each	9ft 0in each	Paired c1914	Combination or twin brake vans.
1555	s3221	SER	10 each	16ft 0in each	9ft 0in each	Converted in 1922	For Whitstable Harbour branch.
1557	s1063 and s1065	SER	13 (uprated)	16ft 0in	9ft 0in	Converted in 1922	For Whitstable Harbour branch.
1558	s1062	SER/ SECR	20	18ft 1in	5ft + 5ft	1898-1914	1898-1909 vans with one open verandah.
1559	s2139/8	SECR	25	24ft 0in	16ft 0in	1918/21	On 12in underframe. More built by SR.
1560	None	SR	25	24ft 0in	16ft 0in	1923-7	On 15in underframe. All built by SR.

'Road' brake vans had side doors and could be used for carriage of small consignments or parcels traffic to wayside stations, supervised by the train guard. This practice was fairly common on the more rural branch lines. Some of these vehicles were converted to 'roader' vans from 1910 onwards. These were stripped of their internal guard's accommodation and had an external handbrake provided. As covered goods wagons they were then used on specific services until circa 1922. Some passenger guards vans were also utilised for similar duties. None were allocated SR numbers in 1923, although several were awaiting breaking up at Ashford at this time.

The four 6-ton vehicles withdrawn in 1924 appear to be early examples of diagram 1553, although they were not allocated any Southern Railway diagram number. At least one SR register gives their diagram as 1552, but the authors believe this to be incorrect. They were allocated to specific services from around 1910 onwards and these details were stencilled on the vehicles concerned. Unlike the 'roader' vans, they retained their brake van status throughout.

Diagrams 1554/5/7 were all conversions and rebuilds from the standard diagram 1553 vehicles and are described with these vans on pages 108-12.

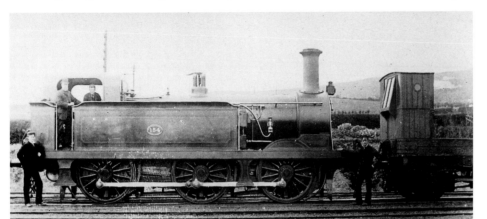

Left:
Plate 137 'R' class 0-6-0T No 154 at Folkestone Junction in 1894, coupled to 'Harbour Bank Brake' No 1999, which was built in 1873. Note the lettering 'SER 1999' on the top side plank and 'FOLKESTONE' on the lower plank. SER livery is a moot point — was it ordinary wagon red or brake van dark reddish brown with bright red ends? The same could be debated of SR livery — were the ends Venetian red? The design dates back to 1855, without any covered booth for the guard. This was later added and four (later three) of these unusual vehicles served the branch until the 1930s. *L&GRP*

Centre left:
Plate 138 The same van in SR days, now renumbered as 55360 and finished in goods wagon livery, coupled to 'R' class 0-6-0T No 153, about 1928. Note that the small round side window has been planked over and the brake gear has been modernised. This van was scrapped in 1936. *Authors' Collection*

Below left:
Plate 139 Every goods or mineral train working up or down the branch had to have at least one 'Harbour Bank Brake' at the seaward end. For loads in excess of seven wagons, two vans had to be provided. The load limit was just 11 wagons, plus two brake vans.

The oldest of the four vans, SER No 2144 (built 1865), lasted until 1951 at Topsham Quay in Devon. As SR No 55363 it was transferred to the South West in 1924, after a runaway accident when five wagons landed in the River Exe.

SR No 55361, formerly SER No 2142, is seen at Folkestone Harbour in June 1931, in what appears to be passenger stock green livery. On the original print the lettering is gilt, shaded in black, with the words 'Southern Railway' appearing in full along the top plank. Built in 1870, this van ran until late 1936. *F. J. Agar*

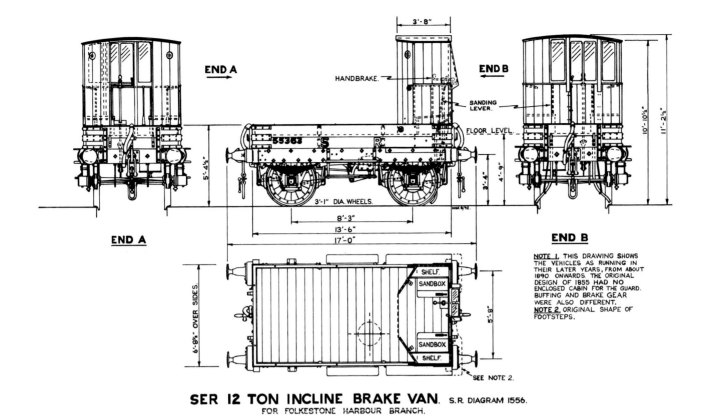

END A →

HANDBRAKE.

SANDING LEVER.

FLOOR LEVEL.

3'-8"

END A

END B

10'-10½"

11'-2½"

5'-4½"

3'-4"

4'-9"

55363 S R

3'-1" DIA. WHEELS.

8'-3"

13'-6"

17'-0"

END A

END B

6'-8½" OVER SIDES.

SHELF.

SANDBOX

SANDBOX

SHELF.

5'-8"

SEE NOTE 2.

NOTE 1. THIS DRAWING SHOWS THE VEHICLES AS RUNNING IN THEIR LATER YEARS, FROM ABOUT 1890 ONWARDS. THE ORIGINAL DESIGN OF 1855 HAD NO ENCLOSED CABIN FOR THE GUARD. BUFFING AND BRAKE GEAR WERE ALSO DIFFERENT.
NOTE 2. ORIGINAL SHAPE OF FOOTSTEPS.

SER 12 TON INCLINE BRAKE VAN. S.R. DIAGRAM 1556.
FOR FOLKESTONE HARBOUR BRANCH.

Above:
Figure 50 The Folkestone Harbour Bank brake van to SR diagram 1556. SER numbers were 1999 and 2142-4. They were seldom seen elsewhere until No 55363 was sent to the Topsham Quay branch in 1924.

Below:
Figure 51 This figure is a drawing of the later type of LCDR goods brake van, as built from 1874 onwards. The LCDR to SECR renumbering lists 74 vehicles in service in 1899, all except five being of 10 tons tare. LCDR numbers were 201-50 and 2201-24, of which at least four (Nos 203/5/6/7) were ballast brakes, described on pages 138 and 145, but most of the others were as shown below. Withdrawal commenced soon after 1899 and was completed just prior to the Grouping, many of the former SECR numbers being reallocated to new Maunsell brake vans from 1918 onwards. Only two vans became SR property: one as a match truck to a crane, the other as a departmental sponge cloth van. The latter was SECR No 11904 (ex-LCDR No 239), which dated from 1888. As SR No 0758S, it lasted until 1929, but it is not known how the van was modified for its departmental service. Amongst the last survivors in ordinary traffic were SECR Nos 11917/19/21/6, formerly LCDR Nos 2202/4/6/11. It is not known if they remained on the former Chatham section after 1899 or if they could be seen throughout the SECR system.

LC&DR GOODS BRAKE VAN
NO SR DIAGRAM

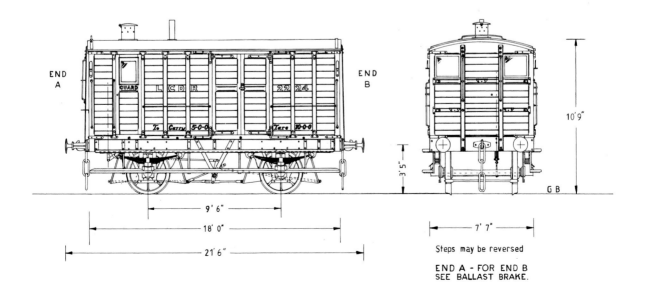

END A

END B

GUARD L C D R S 22 24

To Carry 5-0-0   Tare 10-0-0

9' 6"

18' 0"

21' 6"

10'9"

3' 5"

G B

7' 7"

Steps may be reversed

END A - FOR END B SEE BALLAST BRAKE.

Left:

Plate 140 LCDR brake No 2224 appears behind 'E' class 4-4-0 No 516, which has been posed with three new Pullman cars for an official photograph at Bricklayers Arms in 1910. Pictures of LCDR goods brake vans are remarkably elusive, so this one of a van still in LCDR livery is of particular interest. Considering that over 10 years has elapsed since the last repaint, the lettering and number remain very clear, especially when compared to the generally weathered state of the rest of the van. Perhaps the letters alone have been repainted or cleaned around in the intervening years. In comparison, the lettering on the SER diagram 1553 van alongside appears very weathered. These are of the form SE&CDR, as applied for a very short time in 1899/1900. LCDR No 2224 later became SECR No 11939.
J. H. Kent Collection

Right:

Plate 141 Also at Bricklayers Arms, but circa 1898, is seen an SER 'Express Goods Break' (to use the contemporary spelling). Thirty-two were built between 1885 and 1893 and all are listed in SER records as being 'provided with large wheels, screw couplings and scroll irons and suitable to run in Special or Fast Passenger Trains'. Most had through vacuum pipes but some were fully vacuum fitted. There were minor differences between the various batches, for example those built at Ashford had round-topped lookouts, those by Cravens had flat tops and there were at least two styles of brake rigging: one with four brake blocks and one with eight brake blocks.
The Boys Own Railway Book

Below:

Figure 52 The SER express good brake van, to SR diagram 1552.

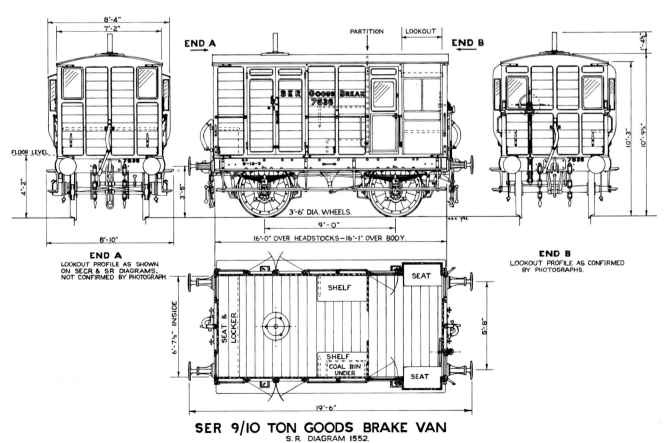

SER 9/10 TON GOODS BRAKE VAN
S. R. DIAGRAM 1552.

Plate 142 This interesting comparison of two goods brake vans was taken at Faversham about 1903. To the left is an anonymous diagram 1552 van, whilst on the right is one of the 'Midland-style' vans to diagram 1558, but in original condition with one open and one enclosed end. It is still in SER livery, so must be one of the original batch numbered between 2005 and 2014. Further details of these vans may be found on pages 112-117. The Kent & East Sussex Railway is fortunate to have one of each of these vans in its collection. *Dr Evers, courtesy R. L. Ratcliffe*

Plate 143 Cable-laying work for the forthcoming Eastern Section electrification scheme is in progress, at Elmstead Woods during the winter of 1924/5. 'R1' class 0-6-0T No 340, from Bricklayers Arms shed, is in charge of the train which includes diagram 1552 brake van No 1677, allocated SR No 55188 but scrapped in September 1926 probably before being renumbered. It was built in 1889 and was one of 12 such vans to survive the Grouping. SR numbers were 55187-9 and 55351-9, but it is doubtful if many were ever renumbered or repainted in SR livery. What was probably the last survivor, SER No 2483, was withdrawn in July 1928 and the body was then grounded within Ashford Wagon Works. It was moved to a garden in Ashford about 1970 and more recently on to the Kent & East Sussex Railway, where at the time of writing it awaits restoration. *Ian Allan Library*

Left:
Plate 144 SER passenger brake vans of the period were very similar to the goods brake vans, but were 18ft long. Some of these became 'roader' vans or departmental stock in their later years, as typified by SR No 138S at Newhaven in 1932. Built as long ago as July 1851, as passenger brake No 45, it later became a breakdown van at Tonbridge Loco, moving to Newhaven in 1929. It shows the 'slide' brake, so named because the four brake blocks moved horizontally along the metal bar visible between the axleboxes. The guard's door is also adjacent to the end of the van and this feature was also found on very early examples of SECR diagram s1063, although the authors have yet to find a photograph of one of these vans.
H. F. Wheeller

Centre left:
Plate 145 An early example of diagram 1553, the standard SER 16ft goods brake van is seen at Grove Park around 1900. This illustrates a typical feature of SECR goods train operation, namely the use of a brake van at both ends of the train. The van itself has only four brake blocks and curved ends to the headstocks, typical of vehicles built between 1879 and 1883. The early vans do not appear to have been provided with roof ventilators. Also seen is a dumb-buffered coal wagon, of a type later to become SR diagram 1328.
R. L. Ratcliffe Collection

Below left:
Plate 146 LCDR 'M2' class 4-4-0 No 643 at Faversham, circa 1910, with a train of two Cotton Powder Co gunpowder vans and a diagram 1553 goods brake van. The latter is possibly SECR No 6352, built in 1879, and is provided with slide brakes and four brake blocks. Note that an additional side vent is fitted between the two doors. This van was withdrawn in 1911. Faversham was an important centre for the gunpowder industry.
Courtesy Fleur de Lis Heritage Centre, Faversham

Right:

Plate 147 One of a batch of 12 vans completed at Ashford in 1896, SER No 1880 is pictured finished in what is presumed to be reddish-brown livery with bright red ends. The lettering is white, with black shading, but not all body ironwork is picked out in black. This van failed to become SR stock in 1923 but SER Nos 1879/82 from the batch did survive as SR Nos 55204/5. Note the two different sizes of torpedo ventilators — that over the luggage compartment is 4in in diameter whilst the one over the guard's section is only 3in in diameter. The recorded cost of this van was £152. *SER Official*

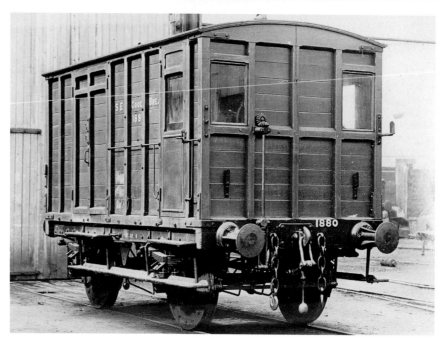

Right:

Plate 148 The same van, showing the guard's compartment end, with the slightly different window arrangement. Note the spelling 'Break'. This was altered to 'Brake' after 1900. Also provided are screw couplings, safety chains and eight brake blocks. The brake wheel, bevel gears and brake rodding are also conspicuous. The stepboards are not full length — vans built prior to 1900 had short stepboards, those built later had full-length ones. Compare the livery with the Gloucester-built van shown in **Plate 8**. *SER Official*

Left:

Plate 149 Another van from the 1879-83 period, SECR No 6357 at Queenborough between 1900 and 1910, when the vehicle was taken out of traffic. It was one of 12 built by Cravens in 1879, but eight similar vans were also completed at Ashford at the same time. Some of these were rated at 9 instead of 10 tons. Note the lettering style, viz:

SE & CR
GOODS 6357 BRAKE.

It has no roof vents and has the usual four brake blocks and slide brake, plus the curved headstock ends. Vans built after 1883 had vertical headstock ends, flush with the body framing. Notice the freshly repainted roof, although the rest of the van is somewhat weathered. *Edwards Bros*

109

Above:
Plate 151 Maunsell-era lettering is carried by van No 11891, photographed in 1921. This was built in 1903 as a replacement for an ex-LCDR van and later became SR No 55272. The diagonal door bracing was a common addition from about 1915 onwards. The picture is endorsed 'Old yard H. Heath', presumably referring to Haywards Heath, but the reason why the van is on the LBSCR is not known.
R. Merry-Price Collection

Above:
Plate 150 An interesting picture of a goods train guard posing in front of his van. Unfortunately, neither the date nor the location is recorded, but the chalked lettering on the door appears to read 'Dunton Green'. On the original print the van number is just visible as 119XX, one of a large order for 80 vans placed with the Metropolitan Railway Carriage & Wagon Co in 1900/1, SECR numbers being 11981-2060. Note the different style of buffer and spoke, instead of the usual Mansell wheels. In the late 1930s van No 55274 was lettered 'To Work Between Dunton Green and Tonbridge Only'. In the 1930s several of these vans were allocated to specific duties, a few examples being:
No 55194 — 'To Work Between Bexhill and Hastings Only'.
No 55276 — 'To Work Between Shorncliffe and Adisham Only'.
No 55305 — 'Northfleet — For Local Trips Only'.
R. W. Kidner Collection

Below:
Figure 53 This figure is a drawing of the earliest type of goods brake van covered by SR diagram 1553, although it is not certain if any of this style actually became SR stock in 1923. Vans built after 1878 were 7ft 8in wide, whilst those built prior to this date were 2in narrower. There is also the question of the position of the guard's door and this appears to be an instance where the SECR diagrams are incorrect. SECR diagram s1063 shows a van where the guard's door is adjacent to the end of the van, whilst s1065 shows it in the correct position, separated from the end by a narrow panel. The latter arrangement is confirmed by all known photographs; however, the SECR register at the PRO at Kew records all vans as diagram s1063. Diagram s1065 appears to have been used only for the 'roader' conversions. The authors believe that the four 6-ton vans withdrawn in 1924 were as shown below, but cannot be absolutely certain. Likely SECR Nos were 4763-7, 4956-66, 5069-78, 5423/4, 5927-30 and 6186/7, built 1869-78.

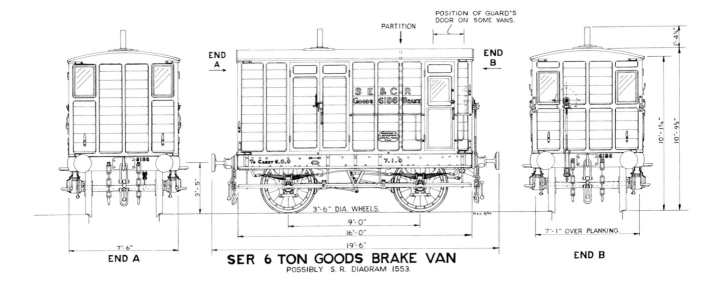

SER 6 TON GOODS BRAKE VAN
POSSIBLY S. R. DIAGRAM 1553.

Left:

Plate 152 Another van from the Metropolitan 1900/1 order, SR No 55339, at Bournemouth in September 1933. It is boarded 'To Work Between Bournemouth Central Goods Yard, Boscombe and Bournemouth Central Loco'. Formerly SECR No 12047, it lasted until July 1935. Few ex-SECR brake vans were seen on the SW section, but SR Nos 55209/18 were noted from 1933 at Eastleigh, lettered up 'Eastleigh — Local Trips Only'. *H. F. Wheeller*

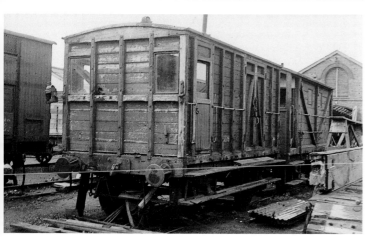

Left:

Plate 153 The last van built to this design (apart from one fire-damage replacement) was also the last survivor. SECR No 11927 was completed in November 1903 and ran until March 1943, by then numbered SR 55279. It was then used as a store at Eastleigh Carriage Works, where it was seen in August 1950. From September 1931 it had been boarded 'To Work Between Bexhill and Hastings Only'. *D. Cullum*

Below:

Figure 54 A combined drawing showing the various permutations of SR diagrams 1553/4/5/7. This illustrates the post-1883 design with eight brake blocks.

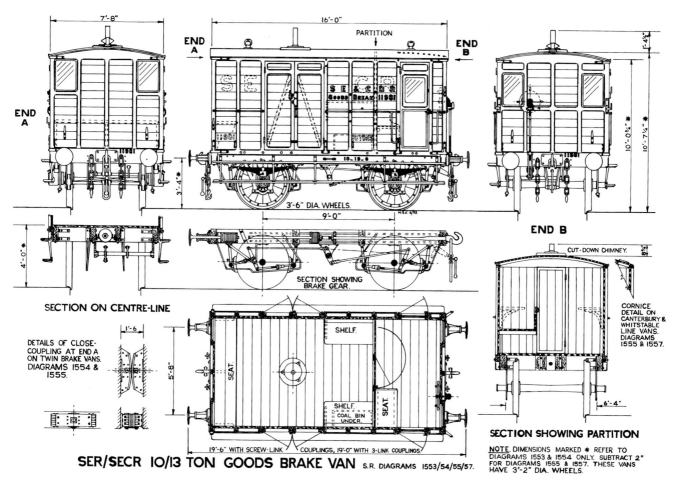

SECTION ON CENTRE-LINE

DETAILS OF CLOSE-COUPLING AT END A ON TWIN BRAKE VANS. DIAGRAMS 1554 & 1555.

SECTION SHOWING BRAKE GEAR.

END B

CUT-DOWN CHIMNEY.

CORNICE DETAIL ON CANTERBURY & WHITSTABLE LINE VANS. DIAGRAMS 1555 & 1557.

SECTION SHOWING PARTITION

SER/SECR 10/13 TON GOODS BRAKE VAN S.R. DIAGRAMS 1553/54/55/57.

NOTE. DIMENSIONS MARKED * REFER TO DIAGRAMS 1553 & 1554 ONLY. SUBTRACT 2" FOR DIAGRAMS 1555 & 1557. THESE VANS HAVE 3'-2" DIA. WHEELS.

Right:
Plate 154 A special goods train comprising 'C' class 0-6-0 No 262, a SECR type-C horsebox, a GWR four-plank open goods and what appears to be a twin brake (or Combination Brake, as they were officially known) to SR diagram 1554 at the rear. The location is not recorded, but the date is circa 1915. The single 10-ton brake vans were too light for the heavier goods trains in later years, so the company fitted up at least seven pairs of these twin brakes after 1914, so that they could be controlled by one guard. They were coupled together with the guard's compartments outward, using the same cast-iron block and pin coupling as used on the twin bolster wagons. The brake rodding was so arranged that all 16 brake blocks could be applied from either van, the Appendix to the *Goods Working Timetable* informing the staff 'that considerably more screwing on of the brake is necessary'. Two pairs of these vans were cut down in 1922 for use on the Canterbury and Whitstable line and these had vacuum pipes and sanding gear added. The guard's doors were also modified to open inwards — a modification applied to many of the standard vehicles. The other five pairs remained in general service, but were hand braked only. Operationally they were considered the equivalent of a 20-ton brake and could be used accordingly. However, all were withdrawn from traffic by 1928, so presumably they were not entirely successful.
R. S. Carpenter Collection

Two ordinary vans (SECR Nos 8930 and 11991) were uprated to 13 tons in about 1914. The additional tare weight allowed them to be used on goods trains of up to 39 loaded wagons, whereas the 10-tonners were restricted to 30 loaded wagons. The 1917 *Goods Working Timetable* lists regular workings for these two vans, encompassing the Sheerness branch, Strood and Faversham. Although useful, no others were uprated and in 1922 both were cut down for use on the Canterbury & Whitstable branch, eventually becoming the only examples to SR diagram 1557. Both were withdrawn in 1928, being replaced on the branch by three modified LSWR diagram 1541 vehicles. Numbering details of all the 16ft brake vans are given below, starting with the combination brakes.

SECR Nos	SR Nos	SECR Nos	SR Nos	SECR Nos	SR Nos
1682+1685	55195+55197	11992+12019	55287+55312	12018+12050	55311+55342
11982+11983	55281+55282	*12008+12031	*55302+55324	*12042+12045	*55334+55337
11984+12038	55283+55330				

*Cut down for Canterbury & Whitstable branch in 1922

SER/SECR Nos	Survivors to SR Nos	SR Diagram	Date Built	Remarks
5076	Allocated 55185	None	Ashford 1872	Allocated to work with gas tanks.
5423/4	Allocated 55183/4	None	Ashford 1874	Allocated to work with gas tanks.
6186	Allocated 55186	None	Ashford 1878	Allocated to mail traffic between Maidstone West & Bricklayers Arms.
1677/89/92/4	55188 only	1552	Ashford 1889	No 1677/55188 with vacuum brake.
2483, 6297	55189 only	1552	Ashford 1889	No 2483/55189 now on K&ESR.
1675, 1684	None	1552	Ashford 1893	Both condemned in 1922.
7531-42	55351-7	1552	Ashford 1885	11 to capital a/c, one to renewal a/c.
7747-56	55187/55358 only	1552	Cravens 1887	With flat-topped lookouts.
7757/8	55359 only	1552	Ashford 1887	On renewal account.
1674/6/8-83, 1685/6	55190-8	1553/4	Ashford 1893	Two later modified to diagram 1554.
1873-87	55199-208	1553	Ashford 1896	
2000-4	55209-13	1553	Ashford 1898	
2015-19	55214-8	1553	Ashford 1899	
3042-61	55219-33	1553	Metrop 1900	
3062-71	55234-43	1553	Ashford 1900	No 3065 'reconstructed' in 1905.
6292-6	None	1553?	Ashford 1878/9	Probably to this design.
6348-55	None	1553	Ashford 1879	Some to 'roader' vans from 1910.
6356-67	55244-8	1553	Cravens 1879	Some to 'roader' vans from 1910.
6545-54	55249-51	1553	Cravens 1881	Some to 'roader' vans from 1910.
7296-8	55252-3	1553	Ashford 1883	
8930-49	55254-69 and 55364 (13 tons)	1553/7	Gloucester 1898	With spoke wheels. No 8930/55364 later to diagram 1557.
11883/90/1, 11912/15/17/19, 11921/6/7	55270-9	1553	Ashford 1903	Replacements for LCDR stock.
11981-2060	55280-350 and 55365 (13 tons)	1553/4/5/7	Metropolitan 1900/1	Twelve later to diagram 1554, four of these subsequently to dia 1555. No 11991/55365 later dia 1557.

Right:
Plate 155 In 1898 the SER built the first of its 'Midland Railway-style' brake vans. The order describes them as a 'special type'. In time, they were to become the standard SECR heavy goods brake van for main line services. Those built from 1898-1909 had one open and one enclosed verandah. One of these is seen near Redhill, in the company of a solitary open goods wagon to diagram 1327. Note the freshly repainted side panel, covering the original SER lettering. *L&GRP*

Above:
Plate 156 A serious rear-end collision occurred at Paddock Wood on 5 May 1919. Three diagram 1558 vans were damaged, but all were repaired and returned to traffic. No 2033 in the foreground has two enclosed verandahs and Maunsell lettering, whilst the van in the background is in original condition with the Wainwright lettering layout. *Authors' Collection*

Right:
Plate 157 1908-vintage brake van No 2036 is seen with newly converted electric stock at Redhill in 1925. The lettering now omits the words 'Goods Brake' from the side panels. *Authors' Collection*

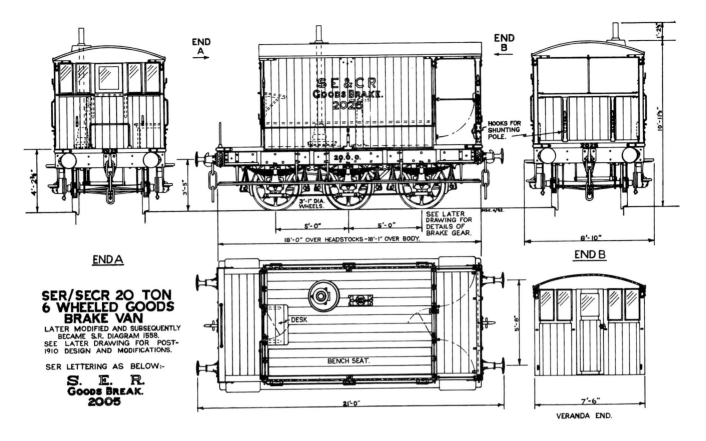

END A

**SER/SECR 20 TON
6 WHEELED GOODS
BRAKE VAN**

LATER MODIFIED AND SUBSEQUENTLY
BECAME S.R. DIAGRAM 1558.
SEE LATER DRAWING FOR POST-
1910 DESIGN AND MODIFICATIONS.

SER LETTERING AS BELOW:-

**S. E. R.
GOODS BREAK.
2005**

END B

VERANDA END.

Above and below

Figures 55 and 56 These figures show the original 1898 and later 1910 design of diagram 1558. Forty vans were completed as above, with one open and one enclosed balcony or verandah, whilst 50 more were built fully enclosed as shown below. The earlier vans were then modified with two enclosed balconies between 1914 and 1920. There were several detail differences between the various batches, including at least two types of stove, handrails, window bars and security arrangements, plus more modern axleboxes on those vans completed in 1914. All 90 vans became SR stock and the majority passed into British Railways ownership. The most obvious difference between the pre and post-1909 vehicles, once rebuilt, concerns the balcony end framing. Those rebuilt had a double top rail at the rebuilt end only whereas those built new with two enclosed balconies had a single rail at both ends. There were also minor differences to the side framing at cantrail level, which are described in subsequent photographs. Full numbering details may be found on page 118.

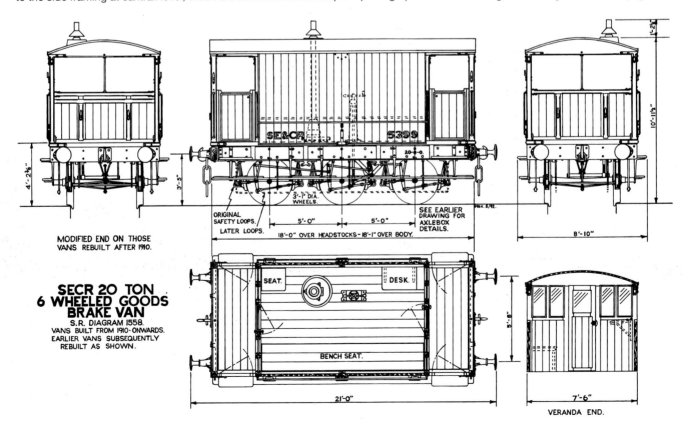

MODIFIED END ON THOSE
VANS REBUILT AFTER 1910.

**SECR 20 TON
6 WHEELED GOODS
BRAKE VAN**

S.R. DIAGRAM 1558.
VANS BUILT FROM 1910 ONWARDS.
EARLIER VANS SUBSEQUENTLY
REBUILT AS SHOWN.

VERANDA END.

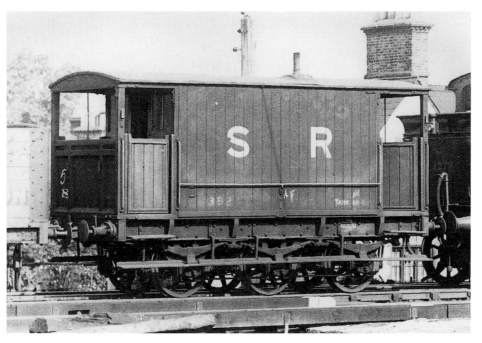

Left:
Plate 158 SR No 55382 wears standard 1930s livery at Redhill in August 1932. This was built in December 1906 as SECR No 2028, with one open and one enclosed balcony. The open end was to the left, the double top rail to the new balcony being visible. Note also the different detail at the inner ends of the two verandahs, just below the roof line. On the right is a metal 'tee' strap, which is absent at the left-hand end. This van remained in traffic until August 1949.
*H. C. Casserley, courtesy
R. M. Casserley*

Below:
Plate 159 The last van to be built, SECR No 5271, photographed at Ashford Works in June 1948, by then renumbered as S55405. This was completed in August 1914 with two enclosed balconies — note the similarity of the roof line detail at the inner ends of both verandahs. Both ends are also the same. This van differs from most of the others illustrated in having more modern axleboxes and an alternative type of stove. Externally this is only obvious due to the chimney, with a conical cowl instead of the usual plain stove pipe. Livery is SR brown with Venetian red ends but with the company initials replaced by the 'S' prefix to the number. The metal plate along the lower edge of the bodywork was an easy way to cover the rotting ends of the vertical side planking. Withdrawal came in 1952. *National Railway Museum*

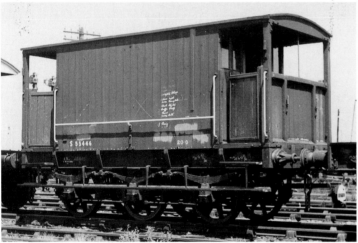

Above:
Plate 160 SR post-1936 lettering is carried by No 55384 at Ashford in 1948. Built in January 1907 as SECR No 2030, it ran until 1951. The original enclosed end is to the left, with the 'tee' strapping clearly visible. *E. B. Trotter*

Left:
Plate 161 Also at Ashford, in June 1951, No S55446 was one of 10 built by Brown Marshall in 1900/1. Originally SECR No 12061, this ran until 1953. Livery is recorded as brown with red ends. *A. E. West*

Below left:
Plate 162 By the 1950s a few vans could be seen away from the Eastern Section. No S55418 was photographed in 1953, stencilled in italic script 'Internal use only Netley Hospital'. For this duty it had vacuum pipes and sanding gear added in July 1950. Built in June 1912 as SECR No 5399, it forms the subject of **Figure 56** on page 114. The van remained on the Netley Hospital branch until at least October 1955, finally receiving an internal user No in the 08XXXX series.
A. R. Sedgwick

Left:

Plate 163 Probably the last diagram 1558 van in service was No DS55380, seen at Seaton Junction in March 1960. Built in July 1905 as SECR No 2025, it entered the engineer's fleet in January 1950 and was allocated to Redbridge Works, being used with long-welded rail trains. It had vacuum pipes added and could be seen all over the Southern Region until 1965. It should have been painted ED black, but managed to retain its unfitted grey livery to the end.
A. E. West

Left and below :

Plates 164 and 165 Two more detail views of No DS55380, at Axminster in 1960. To the left is a close-up of the rebuilt verandah end while below is the original end detail. Note that the headstocks are formed of steel channels with the flanges outermost, with timber packings within the channels. The buffers are also mounted on oval-shaped packings.
Both A. E. West

The SECR *Goods Working Timetable* for 1917 lists 78 duties for these vans, with the remaining 12 standing spare at Bricklayers Arms, Hither Green, Stewarts Lane and Gillingham. Some main line services required the provision of two vans, one at each end of the train, as seen in the Paddock Wood accident in **Plate 156**. This timetable also included a regular working of one of these vans to Oxford via Reading, extended on occasions as far as Crewe, LNWR. In the reverse direction, one LNWR 20-ton six-wheeled brake van had a regular duty as far as Redhill from Reading. Through workings with GWR brake vans were also a regular occurrence during the wartime period. During World War 1 the SECR found itself short of goods brake vans and some bogie passenger brake thirds and two bogie passenger brake vans were pressed into goods train service in the London area. It also borrowed 10 Hull & Barnsley

12-ton goods brake vans to make good the deficiency. These were boarded 'For use on SECR only'. Evidently the good relationship with that railway had survived from the days of William Kirtley.

Of the 90 examples to diagram 1558, only four failed to become BR stock in 1948. General withdrawal took place between 1949 and 1960, except for those transferred to engineer's stock in 1950. These included DS55380/94, 55419/55. One of the original 1898 vehicles, SR No 55371, was withdrawn in 1955 and then sold to the Royal Aircraft Establishment railway at Farnborough, Hampshire. It was then used on the line's coal trains until 1965 and subsequently purchased by the Kent & East Sussex Railway, where it may be seen at the time of writing. At present, it is in a rather inaccurate SER red oxide livery.

Numbering details for diagram 1558 are given below.

SECR Nos	SR Nos	Date Built	Remarks
2005-14	55366-75	1898/9	Original SER 'special' brake vans.
12061-70	55446-55	1900-1	Built by Brown Marshall & Co Ltd.
2020/1/3-5	55376-80	1905	
2028-32	55382-6	1907	
2033-7	55387-91	1908	Locks and window bars fitted.
2026/38-2041	55381/92-5	1909	Last batch with one open balcony.
5408-22	55426-40	1910/11	First batch with two enclosed balconies.
5395-405/7	55416-25	1912	Not completed in numerical order.
5425-9	55441-5	1912	Not completed in numerical order.
5364-8/91-5	55406-15	1913	
5261-5/7-71	55396-405	1914	Different stoves and axleboxes.
All except Nos 12061-70 were built at Ashford.			

We now come to the last SECR goods brake van — the Maunsell/Lynes 25-ton vehicle of 1918. As usual, this bore no resemblance to previous designs, but was a thoroughly modern van, 24ft long over headstocks with a wheelbase of 16ft. The characteristic semi-elliptical roof profile was provided, giving the van a most stately appearance. It did not leak either, unlike the covered goods van, almost certainly because the brake was more heavily constructed. They were extremely capacious for one man, so in SR days this fact earned them the nickname of 'Dance Halls'. The Southern considered the accommodation to be excessive and produced its own shortened bodywork design, but used the same underframe as the SECR vehicles.

The first van entered service in October 1918, on the 10.30am Grove Park to Tonbridge goods, then running light to Paddock Wood, thence on the 9.10pm Paddock Wood-Richborough and returning on the 2am from Richborough to Chislehurst goods. It was then returned with the locomotive (usually one of Maunsell's new 'N' class 2-6-0s) to Grove Park in time to restart the cycle again. Nineteen more vans followed in 1921, with a further batch of 20 on order at the Grouping. Subsequently, the Southern Railway completed a further lot of 20 in 1926/7, these being built at Lancing Works. Numbering details are as below.

SECR Nos	SR Nos	Date Built	Remarks
11892	55456	1918	On 12in channel u/frame, SR diagram 1559.
11893-903/5-11/13	55457-75	1921	On 12in channel u/frame, SR diagram 1559.
11914/16/18/20/2-5/8-39	55476-95	1923	On 15in channel u/frame, SR diagram 1560. Probably delivered in SR livery.
None	55496-515	1926/7	SR order L110, to SR diagram 1560.

One more batch was ordered in 1923 (SR order A29) but was later cancelled in favour of 20 War Department LSWR-type vans purchased secondhand from Cohen Armstrong Disposal Board in 1924.

Below:
Figure 57 This figure shows both versions of these vans, to diagrams 1559 and 1560.

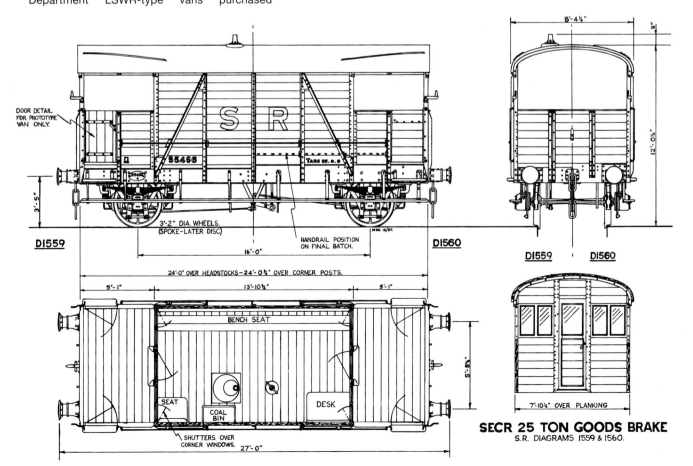

SECR 25 TON GOODS BRAKE
S.R. DIAGRAMS 1559 & 1560.

Above:

Plate 166 The 'pattern' Maunsell/Lynes 25-ton goods brake van, No 11892, carrying a painting date of 10 September 1918. It was booked out of Ashford Works in the following October. This was the first 25-ton goods brake van on the South Eastern — indeed possibly the first in Britain, but the additional tare weight (obtained by infilling the pockets of the 12in channel underframe with scrap metal) was considered necessary when operating heavy unbraked goods trains over the steep gradients encountered on some South Eastern lines. At the first repaint, circa 1921/2, the words 'Goods Brake' were omitted. This van was slightly different to all production examples in having vertically-planked balcony doors, referred to in SR days as 'gates', a feature it retained throughout its long life. The subsequent SR number was 55456 and it remained in service for over 60 years. Many of these vans lasted until the 1970s, by then in engineer's department use. *SECR Official*

Left:

Plate 167 The 'pattern' van again, now numbered S55456, at Templecombe in May 1953. Note that it is now boarded 'Not to Work between Tonbridge & West St Leonards via Battle' — a restriction applied to all diagram 1559 and 1560 vans. Also carried is a 'Hither Green Sidings' allocation, but this has not stopped it from wandering into Somerset! From late 1960 it was allocated to the engineer's department at Redbridge. Apart from provision of disc wheels, it appears almost unchanged from its 1918 appearance. *A. E. West*

Centre left:

Plate 168 Vans built from 1923-7 featured a 15in underframe, although the height was unaltered. Notice the omission of the bottom 3in plank compared to earlier vans. No S55478 was completed in November 1923, so may not have carried its allocated SECR number, 11918. It is seen at its 'home' depot of Eastleigh in 1962, finished in ED black livery with yellow lettering. Several of these vans are now in the hands of preservation societies and a few now carry SECR grey livery with bright red ends. As discussed at the beginning of this chapter, this may be historically inaccurate. *A. E. West*

Below left:

Plate 169 Ten vans were rebuilt in November 1953 to provide riding accommodation for permanent way staff. SR numbers were 55476/82/6/9/92-4/9, 55502/8, all from diagram 1560. These were allocated diagram 1761. One balcony was incorporated into the van section, side and end windows being added. No DS55508 is seen at its 'home' depot, New Cross Gate in 1954. All these were vacuum fitted and some received air pipes in the 1970s, enabling them to remain in service into the 1980s. *A. Blackburn*

Chapter 7.
Bolster and Timber Wagons

Less than 300 bolster, timber and batten wagons were passed to the Southern Railway at the Grouping — a very small total. However, they were made up of at least nine different types, with variations, as listed below.

SR Diagram	SECR Diagram	Origin	Capacity (tons)	Length Over Headstocks	Wheel-base	Known Period of Construction	Remarks
1601	s481	LCDR	6 and 8	13ft 6in	7ft 0in	1879-96	Short bolster
-	s482	LCDR	7, 8 and 10	16ft 0in	9ft 0in	1875-99	Long bolster
1602	s5199	SER	8 each	13ft 0in each	7ft 0in each	Paired 1920/1	Twin bolsters
1603	s480	SER	8	13ft 0in	7ft 0in	1897-1900	Single bolster
1604	s484	SECR	8	23ft 0in	12ft 0in	1902-12	Double bolster
1605	s483	SECR	10	16ft 0in	9ft 0in	1912-13	Single bolster
1606	s487	SECR	10 each	15ft 0in each	8ft 0in each	1907	Twin bolsters
1607	s486	SECR	10 each	15ft 0in each	8ft 0in each	1911	Twin bolsters
1608	s485	SECR	10 each	16ft 0in each	9ft 0in each	1913	Twin bolsters
1609	s2139/6	SECR	12 each	17ft 0in each	9ft 6in each	1919	Twin bolsters
1610	s2522/8	SECR	12 each	17ft 0in each	9ft 6in each	1921-2	Twin bolsters

In some instances the twin bolsters were identical to some singles, save for the coupling arrangements. For example, diagrams 1602 and 1603 were the same, whilst diagram 1605 and 1608 shared a common base design. Two older types of single bolster wagon failed to become SR stock at the Grouping. The LCDR had some vehicles 12ft 6in long which dated back to 1862, whilst the SER version was a diminutive example only 10ft 0in over headstocks, with a wheelbase of as little as 6ft 0in. These dated back to at least 1882 and probably much earlier, especially as many were equipped with dumb-buffers. That said, however, 10 1897 examples to diagram 1603 were also built with dumb-buffers.

Right:
Plate 170 This view of Dover Priory, probably taken in 1876, includes several single bolster wagons in the foreground. Most prominent is long bolster No 296, one of 16 built in 1875. Behind this are three short bolsters, probably 12ft 6in long, but this cannot be confirmed. A selection of other LCDR locomotives, carriages and wagons may also be seen. Prior to Longhedge C&W Works being opened in 1862, much of the LCDR rolling stock was maintained here. Note also the open goods wagon in the foreground, covered with tarpaulin sheet No 249. *Authors' Collection*

Left:
Figure 58 A drawing of the second type of LCDR short single bolster wagon.

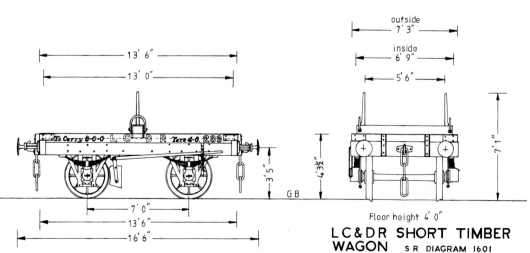

LC&DR SHORT TIMBER WAGON SR DIAGRAM 1601

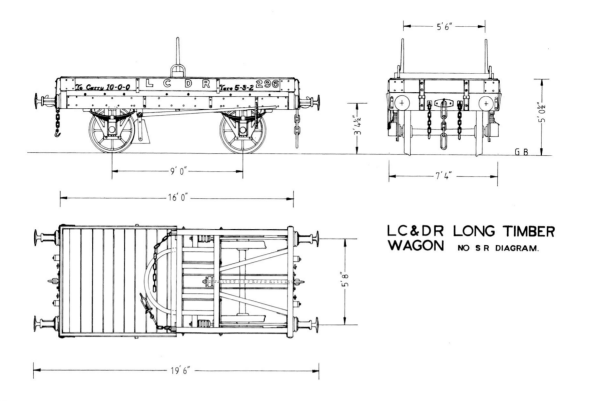

LC&DR LONG TIMBER WAGON NO S R DIAGRAM.

Above:

Figure 59 An example of the LCDR long single bolster wagon, as built from 1875 onwards. None survived as bolster wagons at the Grouping, but at least nine were rebuilt as shunting trucks between 1912 and 1917. Details of these may be found on page 135.

Some numbering details for LCDR bolster wagons are as follows:

Short Single Bolster (Diagram 1601)			Long Single Bolster (No SR Diagram)		
LCDR Nos	SECR Nos	SR Nos	LCDR Nos	SECR Nos	Date Built
255/66/83	11596/607/24	58056, 57931/2	285-300*	11626-41	1875
These three vehicles were the only short			2101-10	11642-51	1877
bolsters to be allocated SR numbers			2111-28	11652-69	1882
*Some vehicles in this batch were replaced by identical vehicles built between 1891 and 1899.					

Right:

Plate 171 A picture included as much for atmosphere as for the wagons. It shows Strood Dock at some time around 1910-12. Dredging works appear to be in progress, with a sailing barge belonging to the firm of Thomas of Rochester in attendance. In the background are, from right to left, a diagram 1553 brake van, two diagram 1420/2 vans, then several open wagons. In the centre, above the dredger's cab, is a dumb-buffered bolster wagon, from the batch numbered 1900-9, built in 1897. Dimensionally, these were as diagram 1603.

Fine Art Studio, Rochester

Left:
Plate 172 One of the 10ft 0in-long SER single bolsters, No 6159, is seen at East Croydon in the spring of 1912. Built in 1890 at a cost of £29 17s 5d, it was withdrawn some time before the Grouping. It illustrates the usual lettering layout for these vehicles. Note the tare weight of less than 3½ tons. Just visible behind is diagram 1328-type coal wagon No 2449. *L. E. Brailsford*

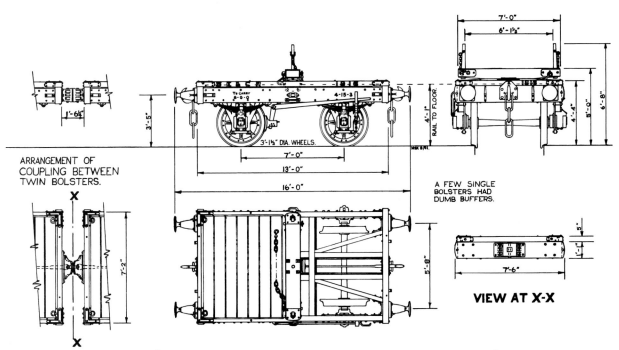

ARRANGEMENT OF
COUPLING BETWEEN
TWIN BOLSTERS.

A FEW SINGLE
BOLSTERS HAD
DUMB BUFFERS.

VIEW AT X-X

SER/SECR 8 TON SINGLE & TWIN BOLSTER WAGONS
S.R. DIAGRAMS 1602 (SINGLE) & 1603 (TWIN).

Above:
Figure 60 A drawing of the SER 13ft 0in single bolster to diagram 1603. One hundred were built between 1897 and 1900, as follows:

SER Nos	Survivors to SR Nos	Date Built
1900-9*	None	Ashford 1897
1910-19	57933-8	Ashford 1898
1960-9	57939-45	Ashford 1899
2870-89†	57946-65	Ashford 1900
8880-929	57966-8007	Bristol W&C Co 1897/8
*With dumb-buffers.		
†With screw couplings.		

In 1920/1, 44 of these wagons were converted into twin bolsters, using block and pin couplings. However, at least 47 wagons were involved as there were several later alterations to the pairings. At least one wagon eventually reverted to a single bolster. It seems that few were ever renumbered or repainted in SR livery, since the SR Registers quote their SECR numbers right up to withdrawal in the early 1930s. Some sample pairings were 8880+8894, 8884+8888, 8886+1910, 8896+2882, 8928+1914 and 2872+2874. The only survivors in 1933 were (all singles) 57949, 57976 and 57997.

Left:

Plate 173 Between 1902 and 1912 48 double bolsters (or batten) wagons were completed, all at Ashford Works. These were often used in conjunction with the single bolsters for carrying longer loads. Wagon No 1983 was photographed somewhere in the Manchester area about 1919, loaded with round timber. The match wagon just seen to the left is LSWR single bolster No 9922. SECR No 1983 was built in 1905 and later became SR No 58031. *HMRS Collection*

Centre left:

Plate 174 Double bolster No 1950, seen at Ashford about 1924. This has Hill's brake gear on one side only. *G. P. Keen*

Below left:

Plate 175 Similar wagon SR No 58009 (ex-SECR No 1951) at Robertsbridge in 1931, loaded with round timber. This seems to have been their most common load. The wagon dates from May 1909 and ran until June 1933. The original cost is recorded as £136. Hill's brake gear was originally provided on one side only and a second set of freighter brakes was added at a later date. This was one of the wagons with movable bolsters. *H. R. Norman*

Below:

Figure 61 The diagram 1604 double bolster wagon with Stone's either-side brake gear, as fitted to vehicles built in 1902. Numbering details are:

SECR Nos	SR Nos	Built	Brakes
1950-9#	58008-17	1909	H
1970-91	58018-39	1904/5	DB
2890-5	58040-5	1902	ST
3206-15#	58046-55	1912	F
#Fitted with movable bolsters.			

These wagons lasted well into Southern Railway days. One or two were withdrawn in the early 1930s but the last one was not withdrawn until 1947. At least two entered departmental service, Nos 1306S and 1812S being noted.

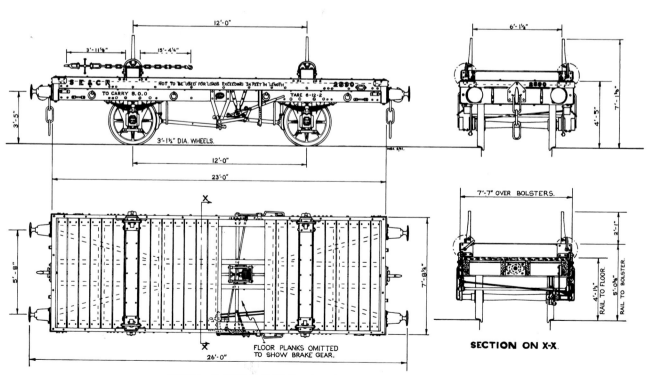

SECR 8 TON DOUBLE BOLSTER WAGON
WITH J. STONE'S EITHER-SIDE BRAKE GEAR. S.R. DIAGRAM 1604.

Left:

Plate 176 From 1907 onwards the SECR favoured twin bolster wagons, ie single bolsters semi-permanently coupled in pairs. Several types were built but only the Maunsell-era ones were well photographed, possibly because the rest had fairly short lives after 1923. At Wimbledon in June 1920 are diagram 1607 pair SECR Nos 6429/30, later allocated SR Nos 58087/8. These date from 1911 and ran until the 1930s. Notice the brake gear — so arranged to give an either-side provision but with only one set per wagon. *H. C. Casserley, courtesy R. M. Casserley*

Most vehicles built new as twin-sets were paired numerically, like the vehicles illustrated above. Those converted subsequent to construction were paired randomly, but some may have swapped partners as necessary. A few were reconverted to single bolsters at a later date, an example being SR No 58069, which was singled in September 1931. It is not known if this modification resulted in a new diagram being issued. Numbering details of these wagons are given below.

SR Diagram	SECR Nos	SR Nos	Remarks
1605	3217-21/5-9	58057-66	Single bolsters. Freighter brake gear.
1606	3971-9/81/2/4-92	58067-86	Hill's brake on one side of each wagon.
			No 58069 single in September 1931.
1607	6429-46	58087-104	Double-block brakes on one side of each wagon.
1608	11647-9/51/3/7/9-64/6-9	58105-20	Double-block brakes on one side of each wagon.

All these wagons were built utilising LCDR wheels, springs and axleboxes.
Most were withdrawn by 1939, but SR Nos 58119/20 lasted until 1951.

Below:
Figure 62 A combined drawing showing all four variations of Wainwright single/twin bolsters.

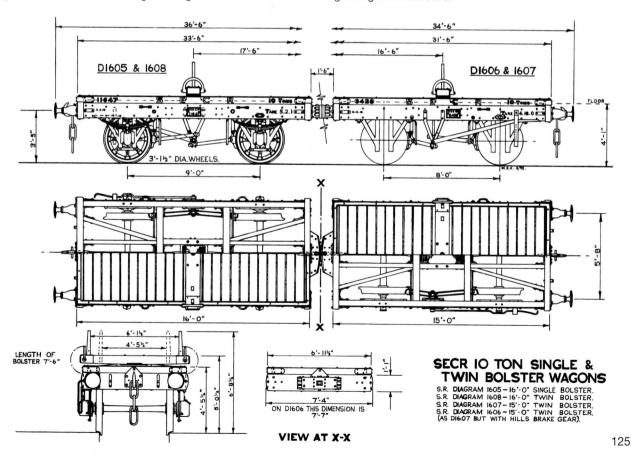

LENGTH OF BOLSTER 7'-6"

ON D1606 THIS DIMENSION IS 7'-7"

VIEW AT X-X

SECR 10 TON SINGLE & TWIN BOLSTER WAGONS
S.R. DIAGRAM 1605 – 16'-0" SINGLE BOLSTER.
S.R. DIAGRAM 1608 – 16'-0" TWIN BOLSTER.
S.R. DIAGRAM 1607 – 15'-0" TWIN BOLSTER.
S.R. DIAGRAM 1606 – 15'-0" TWIN BOLSTER.
(AS D1607 BUT WITH HILLS BRAKE GEAR).

125

Above:
Plate 177 The Maunsell/Lynes twin bolster design, SECR Nos 1891/2, when new in May 1919. SR diagram 1609 was later allocated. The pair entered traffic in July 1919 and later became SR Nos 58121/2, running until 1956. These utilised the standardised 17ft 0in steel underframe with self-contained buffers at the outer ends, but instead of the usual SECR either-side or lift-link brake gear, each wagon was equipped with double-block brakes on one side only, arranged diagonally opposite. Note the different tare weights for what were, effectively, two identical wagons. They were uprated to 13 tons capacity during World War 2, along with the similar diagram 1610 vehicles. *SECR Official*

Below:
Plate 178 Having tested the prototypes, it was found that the placing of the bolsters directly onto the floor of the wagon made shackling of the loads difficult. Accordingly, the design was revised to allow space under the bolsters and 50 pairs of production wagons were completed in 1921/2, later being allocated SR diagram 1610. SECR Nos 3794/5 (later SR Nos 58155/6) were photographed not long after completion following an incident which had resulted in the load of rails shifting in transit. This pair also lasted until 1956. *BR/OPC Collection*

Above:
Plate 179 The Ashford 1948 series of photographs includes Maunsell twin bolsters Nos S58206/8 (ex-SECR Nos 4000/2), one of the pairs which was not consecutively numbered. These date from December 1921 and ran until at least 1957. Of the 50 pairs, only one set failed to become BR stock in 1948, general withdrawal taking place between 1950 and 1960. One pair passed to the signal engineer at Wimbledon and these were the last survivors of the type on the Southern Region. However, they saw very little use in their final days and could usually be found in the 'back road' at Wimbledon yard. SECR numbering of these vehicles was as follows: 3463-84, 3535-44, 3794-806/37-44, 3906-16/58-64/6-70/93-4005, 4404-14. These became SR Nos 58123-222 in the same order. The majority were paired numerically throughout their lives. *National Railway Museum*

Below:
Figure 63 A combined drawing of both the Maunsell/Lynes twin bolster wagons to SR diagrams 1609 and 1610.

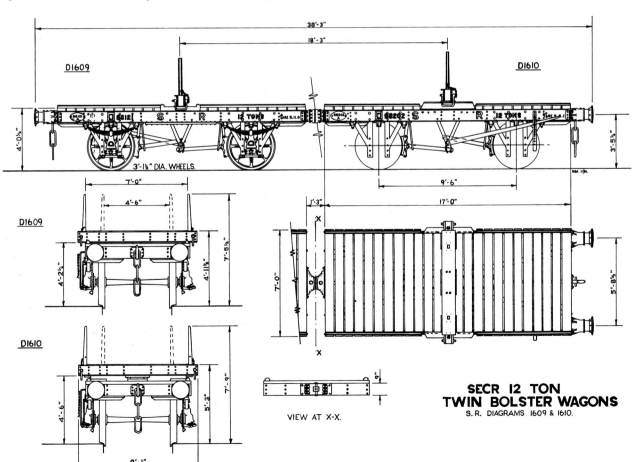

SECR 12 TON
TWIN BOLSTER WAGONS
S. R. DIAGRAMS 1609 & 1610.

VIEW AT X-X.

Chapter 8.
Road Vehicle Trucks

These comprised just four Southern Railway diagrams at the Grouping — a mere 54 wagons. One might be forgiven for thinking that these are fairly straightforward. However, appearances can be deceptive. The SER/SECR vehicles follow fairly standard construction, save for the employment of a steel floor to increase the loading height. The LCDR achieved the same arrangement by insetting the spring hangers into the solebars so that they became invisible when viewed from a horizontal position. To both companies, these wagons were known by the rather colourful title of highway vehicle trucks; the lettering 'For Highway Vehicles' appearing on the side rails throughout the pre-Grouping period. In Southern Railway days they were described as 'Cartrucks'. The four Southern Railway diagrams are listed below, together with the three SECR diagrams of ex-LCDR vehicles extant in 1922, for reasons which will be explained shortly.

SR Diagram	SECR Diagram	Origin	Capacity (tons)	Length Over Headstocks	Wheelbase	Known Period of Construction	Remarks
1654	s1031	SER	8 and 10	16ft 6in	9ft 4in	1886-1900	8ft 2in wide.
1655	s1032	SECR	10	16ft 6in	9ft 4in	1903/6	8ft 4in wide.
1656	(s2514/2)	LCDR	10	17ft 0in	9ft 0in	Rebuilt 1915-17	Diagram dated 1923.
1657	s2139/5	SECR	12	17ft 0in	9ft 6in	1919	Maunsell/Lynes design
–	s1036	LCDR	8 and 10	16ft 6in	9ft 3in	1886-98	3ft 9in to floor.
–	s1079	LCDR	10	16ft 1in	9ft 3in	1877-1883	4ft 2in to floor.
–	Unknown	LCDR	15	19ft 3in	6ft 3in+ 6ft 3in	1891	Six wheels. One wagon only

Diagrams 1654 and 1655 vary only in terms of width and braking arrangements, whilst the Maunsell vehicles never got beyond the 'pattern' wagons. However, diagram 1656 faced the authors with an almost unique challenge. Not only did its printed dimensions fail to agree, but the vehicle drawn did not look anything like any LCDR road vehicle truck known. All we are able to suggest is that someone drew the wrong vehicle back in 1923! For the record, what appears on diagram 1656 is a short, one-plank open which looks like a conversion from a much earlier carriage underframe. It may have either SER or LCDR origins. The length quoted is 17ft over headstocks with a wheelbase of 9ft, plus overhangs of 3ft 3in. This, however, adds up to 15ft 6in, not 17ft as quoted. To cap it all, the drawing scales up at 15ft 6in. Forty-one road vehicle trucks were passed to the SECR from the LCDR in 1899 and just eight remained in stock to become SR property in 1923. Two general arrangement drawings have survived and both are reflected by accurate SECR diagrams. We have therefore used these, plus the evidence of one photograph reproduced on the next page, to illustrate the former LCDR vehicles.

The solitary LCDR six-wheeled vehicle, strictly speaking, does not qualify for inclusion in a book devoted to Southern

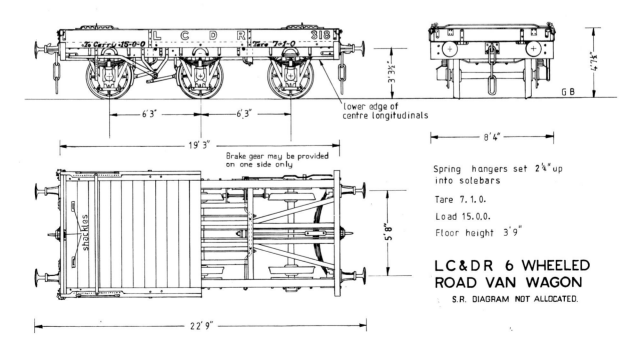

Spring hangers set 2¼" up into solebars

Tare 7. 1. 0.

Load 15. 0. 0.

Floor height 3' 9"

LC&DR 6 WHEELED ROAD VAN WAGON
S.R. DIAGRAM NOT ALLOCATED.

Above:
Figure 64 LCDR six-wheeled road van wagon.

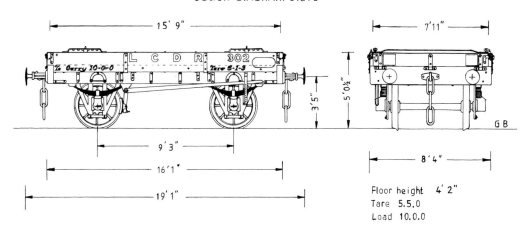

Right:
Figure 65 The standard high-floor LCDR road vehicle truck to SECR diagram s1079. Known numbers are LCDR 302, 329 and 332, later SECR Nos 11941/68/71 and finally SR Nos 60363/7/8.

Floor height 4' 2"
Tare 5.5.0
Load 10.0.0

Railway wagons, since it was withdrawn in August 1922. However, it is a most interesting wagon and indeed was the only one classified as a special wagon by the LCDR. As such, it perhaps warrants inclusion and, maybe, was still awaiting breaking up at Ashford in January 1923 It is reproduced opposite as **Figure 64**. The LCDR number was 318, later

SECR No 11957. Its main duty was the transportation of road/steam rollers and other products of Messrs Aveling & Porter, whose works were adjacent to the SER at Strood. The SER also had vehicles dedicated to this traffic, which are described in Chapter 9.

Left:
Plate 180 Taken at Eastbourne in 1906, low-floor vehicle No 11952 was one of the eight to survive to SR days, being allocated the number 60364. It was LCDR No 313 and was reconstructed at Ashford Works in 1915, finally being withdrawn in November 1923. It had freighter brake gear. LCDR No 314 (SECR No 11953) was similar. The last survivor was SR No 60366, withdrawn in May 1931, formerly SECR No 11963 and LCDR No 324. It is not known if this was a high or low-floor vehicle, nor is it known how many of each design were built. *Authors' Collection*

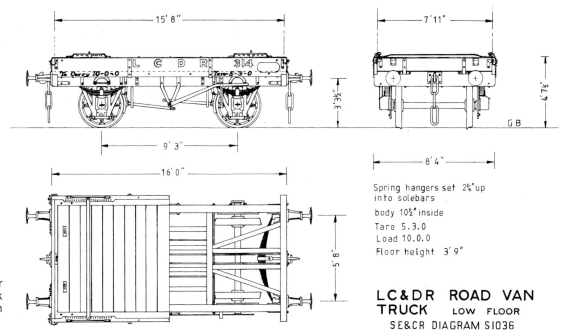

Spring hangers set 2¼" up into solebars
body 10½" inside
Tare 5.3.0
Load 10.0.0
Floor height 3' 9"

Right:
Figure 66 The low-floor LCDR road vehicle truck design to SECR diagram s1036.

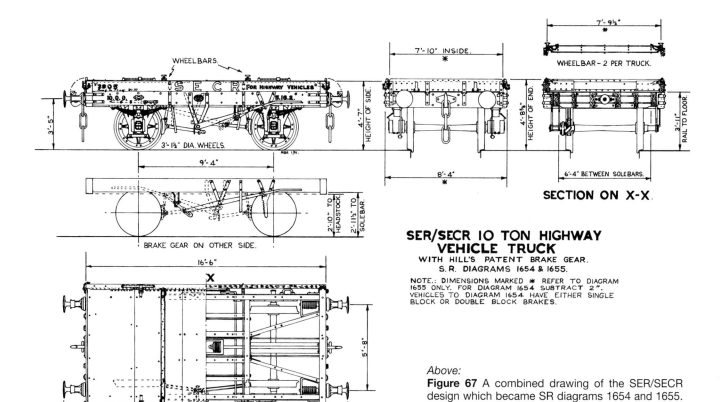

WHEELBARS.

S E C R

FOR HIGHWAY VEHICLES

3'-5"

3'-1½" DIA. WHEELS.

9'-4"

HEIGHT OF SIDE

4'-7"

7'-10" INSIDE.

8'-4"

HEIGHT OF END

4'-8½"

7'-9½"

WHEELBAR - 2 PER TRUCK.

RAIL TO FLOOR.

3'-11"

6'-4" BETWEEN SOLEBARS.

SECTION ON X-X.

BRAKE GEAR ON OTHER SIDE.

2'-10" TO HEADSTOCK

2'-11½" TO SOLEBAR.

16'-6"

X

X

5'-8"

FLOOR PLATES ¾" THICK.

19'-6"

SER/SECR 10 TON HIGHWAY VEHICLE TRUCK
WITH HILL'S PATENT BRAKE GEAR.
S.R. DIAGRAMS 1654 & 1655.

NOTE.: DIMENSIONS MARKED ✱ REFER TO DIAGRAM 1655 ONLY. FOR DIAGRAM 1654 SUBTRACT 2". VEHICLES TO DIAGRAM 1654 HAVE EITHER SINGLE BLOCK OR DOUBLE BLOCK BRAKES.

Above:
Figure 67 A combined drawing of the SER/SECR design which became SR diagrams 1654 and 1655. SER numbers for highway vehicle trucks were all between 3877 and 3908; there was a maximum stock of just 32 wagons at 31 December 1898.

Right:
Plate 181 Twenty-one wagons were built by Hurst Nelson in 1900, SECR Nos being 3321-41. Seventeen survived to become SR stock, numbers being 60319-35. These were to diagram 1654. Wagon No 3325 later became SR No 60322 and lasted until February 1936. Double-block brake gear was fitted originally on one side only, a second set being added in November 1931. Similar SER wagons had single-block brakes, such as No 3888 in **Plate 186** on page 133. *Hurst Nelson & Co*

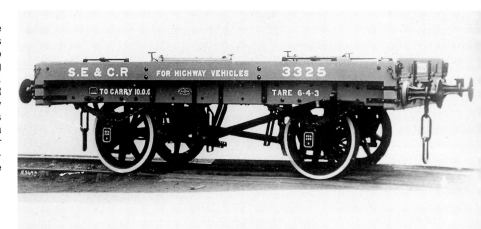

Left:
Plate 182 Between 1903 and 1906 a 2in-wider version was built, later allocated SR diagram 1655. Twenty were completed, in two batches of 10. Hill's brake gear was provided. An anonymous example is seen at Bricklayers Arms some time between 1905 and 1912, loaded with a horse-drawn van belonging to the SECR's local agents, Messrs Joynson's who were contracted to the company to provide cartage in Southeast London. A similar vehicle behind is loaded with a horse lorry. SECR numbers of these vehicles were:

Built 1903 — 3878/89/92/3/5/6, 11956/65-7.
Built 1906 — 3880/7/91, 3905, 11940/3/7/8/59/70.

Those numbered 119XX replaced former LCDR vehicles; the rest replaced ex-SER stock. All were charged to the renewals account. Subsequent SR numbers were 60343-62, in SECR numerical order. The last survivors were withdrawn in the 1940s. *Authors' Collection*

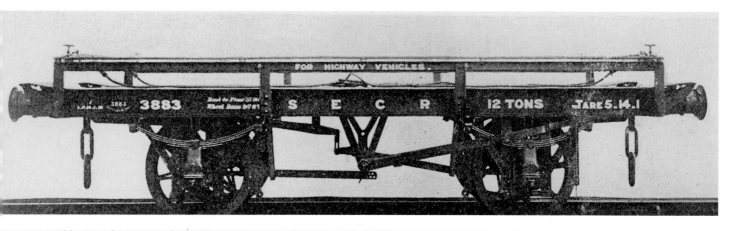

Above:

Plates 183 and 184

The two Maunsell/Lynes vehicles, on the standardised steel underframe, are illustrated on this page. At the *top*, in **Plate 183** we see SECR No 3883 as completed in January 1919, whilst *above* in **Plate 184** the same vehicle appears in the Ashford 1948 series of views, albeit taken in June 1949. By then it was renumbered as S60370, uprated to 13 tons capacity and labelled 'Cartruck'. It was withdrawn in 1956. Fellow vehicle No 3884/60371 was transferred to the outdoor machinery department at Exeter Central in December 1943 and renumbered as 1795S. It was probably repainted in grey livery for this duty.

SECR Official/National Railway Museum

Below:

Figure 68 The Maunsell/Lynes road vehicle truck design of 1919.

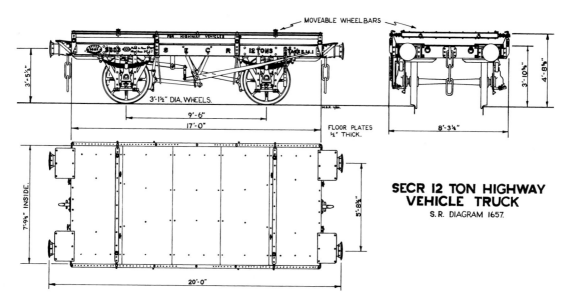

SECR 12 TON HIGHWAY VEHICLE TRUCK
S.R. DIAGRAM 1657.

Chapter 9.
Special Wagons

The vehicles we shall be considering in this section are machinery trucks, shunting trucks, gunpowder vans and aeroplane/platform wagons. The special wagon description is our own, rather than that of the railway companies — indeed the category and actual descriptions varied from one company to another and sometimes from one period to another. For example, the LCDR only classed one wagon as a 'special' — the solitary 15-ton six-wheeled highway vehicle truck, which was described in Chapter 8 — whilst to the South Eastern, the term 'machinery wagon' was foreign — its terminology was 'implement truck'.

It will come as no surprise to the reader that this category was very small — in total less than 60 wagons as at 1 January 1923, comprising seven diagrams. One more design was outstanding at this date but it fell to the Southern Railway to complete the outstanding order, in October 1923. As such, they will be considered as a Southern design and dealt with in Volume 4, but are listed briefly below, together with the seven extant diagrams as at the Grouping.

SR Diagram	SECR Diagram	Vehicle Type	Origin	Capacity (tons)	Length Over Headstocks	Wheel-base	Known Period of Construction	Remarks
1679	s1029	Implement truck	SECR	15	25ft 6in	20ft 0in	1903/13	Two vehicles only. SR code WELL C.
1680	s1030*	Implement truck	SER/SECR	20	20ft 0in	7ft + 7ft	1882-1912	At least nine wagons SR code WELL F.
1681	s3499	Machinery wagon	SECR/SR	20	29ft 6in	22ft 6in	1923-on.	Built by SR. SR code WELL B.
1703	s1056	Gunpowder van	SECR	7	16ft 0in or 16ft 1in	9ft 0in	1899-1900 & 1913	23 vans in three separate batches.
–	s1819	Shunting truck	SER	–	15ft 6in	8ft 6in or 9ft 4in	Rebuilt 1915	Three vehicles only. Ex-SER opens.
–	s2522/1	Shunting truck	LCDR	–	16ft 0in	9ft 0in	Rebuilt 1912-17	Nine vehicles only. Ex-LCDR bolsters.
1101	Unknown	Aeroplane truck	SER	6	40ft 5in	Bogie ccs 25ft 6in	Rebuilt 1917/18	Former coach underframes.
1102	Unknown	Aeroplane truck	SER	6	41ft 11in	Bogie ccs 27ft 0in	Rebuilt 1917/18	Former coach underframes.

*SECR No 1 (later SR No 61047) was purchased from Aveling & Porter and was to diagram s1020. The differences between the two SECR diagrams is not known. The wagon was sold by the SECR in 1912 and repurchased in 1922.

Diagram 1681 is described on both the SECR and SR diagrams as a machinery wagon, so the term implement truck was not in favour at Ashford by 1923. Twelve were completed in 1923 and a further 35 in 1928 and 1942 — by then they were considered as the standard Southern Railway machinery wagon. Prior to the construction of diagram 1681 the most numerous implement trucks were those to diagram 1680. Eleven are listed in SECR registers, but in several instances those running in late SECR days were already replacements for those built in

the 1880s. Some of these took the same running numbers. At least nine were in existence at the Grouping, although two were already in departmental service at Ashford Works and three more were to suffer a similar fate between 1928 and 1930. The final survivors in capital stock were withdrawn in 1935, although at least two of those in service stock lasted until 1938/9. Amongst other duties, they were used to convey the products of Messrs Aveling & Porter to and from their workshops at Strood.

Left:
Plate 185 Taken from Aveling & Porter's catalogue, this view from the early 1900s shows a trainload of traction engines leaving the works. Whilst somewhat retouched, at least four diagram 1680 vehicles are identifiable. One wagon was sold to the company by the SECR in 1912 and repurchased 10 years later for the sum of £70. It is not clear whether the wagon was built new in 1912 or whether it was an older vehicle refurbished for its new owners. On the right is a road vehicle truck of some description. *J. M. Preston Collection*

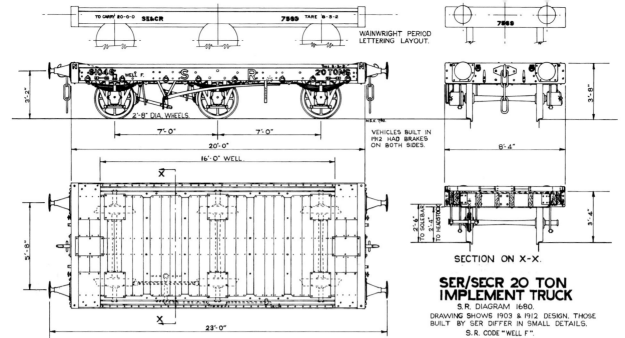

VEHICLES BUILT IN
1912 HAD BRAKES
ON BOTH SIDES.

SECTION ON X-X.

**SER/SECR 20 TON
IMPLEMENT TRUCK**
S.R. DIAGRAM 1680.
DRAWING SHOWS 1903 & 1912 DESIGN. THOSE
BUILT BY SER DIFFER IN SMALL DETAILS.
S.R. CODE "WELL F".

Above:

Figure 69 The 20-ton well wagon/ implement truck to diagram 1680. Known SECR numbers are 1, 1275-7, 1672/3/93/4, 7175 and 7568/9. SECR No 1 was ex-Aveling & Porter's No 1, later SR No 61047.

Right:

Plate 186 Originally published in 1922, this view has been described as being taken at both Lydd and Cambridge! Apart from highway vehicle truck No 3888 (built by the SER in 1897 and later SR No 60337) it shows both vehicles to diagram 1679 (SECR Nos 1671/95, later SR Nos 61039/40), with an unidentified diagram 1680 wagon between them. All are loaded with Aveling & Porter vehicles. *Lens of Sutton*

Below right:

Plate 187 Seen at Walton on Thames in June 1935, is 15-ton implement truck No 61040, loaded with a large transformer. Built in January 1913 as SECR No 1695, it became a departmental yard wagon in July 1946, No 361S. SECR travelling crane and match truck 205S and 205SM are seen behind. These are described in Chapter 11. *F. Foote*

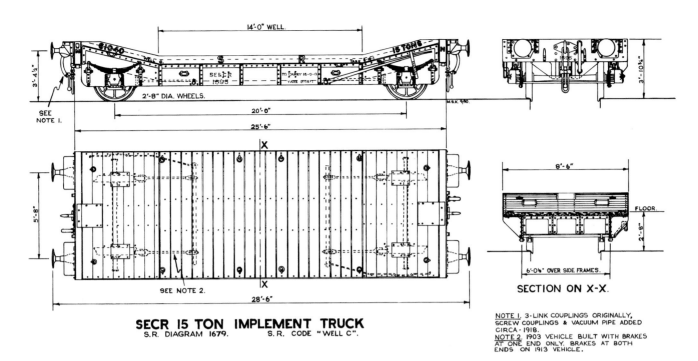

SECR 15 TON IMPLEMENT TRUCK
S.R. DIAGRAM 1679.   S.R. CODE "WELL C".

SECTION ON X-X.

NOTE I. 3-LINK COUPLINGS ORIGINALLY, SCREW COUPLINGS & VACUUM PIPE ADDED CIRCA - 1918.
NOTE 2. 1903 VEHICLE BUILT WITH BRAKES AT ONE END ONLY. BRAKES AT BOTH ENDS ON 1913 VEHICLE.

Above:
Figure 70 The later design of implement truck, to SR diagram 1679. Only two were built and the last survivor in ordinary traffic, No 61039, was withdrawn in 1948.

Left:
Plate 188 At least 12 shunting trucks were converted for use at the larger yards between 1912 and 1917. There were two types, one converted from former SER open goods wagons, the other from ex-LCDR long single bolsters. One of the ex-SER vehicles is visible at Bricklayers Arms circa 1920. The SER van to the left is one of the meat van conversions to diagram 1489.
Authors' Collection

Right:
Plate 189 The Bricklayers Arms shunter, 'S' class 0-6-0ST No 685, coupled to former SER shunting truck No 4795. This was built as long ago as 1869 but was rebuilt as a shunting truck in 1915, along with Nos 4793/4. All three worked at Bricklayers Arms and were first allocated SR departmental service stock numbers 180S-2S. Two were withdrawn in 1923/4, but 181S lasted long enough to receive SR traffic department number 61341 in 1925. It then remained in use until October 1929. It is by no means certain that all three were identical, since official records state the wheelbase to be either 8ft 6in or 9ft 4in. *L&GRP*

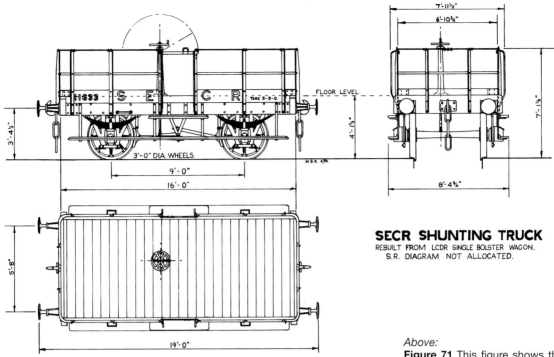

SECR SHUNTING TRUCK
REBUILT FROM LCDR SINGLE BOLSTER WAGON.
S.R. DIAGRAM NOT ALLOCATED.

Above:
Figure 71 This figure shows the former LCDR vehicles, nine of which became SR stock in 1923. They were allocated departmental numbers 183S-191S after the Grouping, but in 1925 those still in use were reallocated traffic stock numbers 61342-48. Their former SECR numbers were 11633/7/9/43/6/50/5/6/65. The last survivor was SR No 61347, scrapped in May 1930.

Left:
Plate 190 Former LCDR shunting truck SR No 61343 at Clapham Junction in May 1928, just three months before withdrawal. This is the only evidence of such a vehicle away from the South Eastern section. Their usual locations were Ashford, Bricklayers Arms and Hither Green, but they may have served at the other large yards on the South Eastern system.
H. C. Casserley, courtesy R. M. Casserley

Right:
Plate 191 The SECR served a number of gunpowder mills and so required a fleet of gunpowder vans. In 1923 this stood at 23 vehicles, but in former years there may have been more, especially during World War 1, when some ordinary covered goods wagons were modified to give temporary additional capacity. This timber-underframed example was photographed at Ashford Works in August 1955, shortly before withdrawal. It was one of a batch of six completed by the SECR in 1899, numbers being 1993-8, later SR Nos 61230-5. These had double-block brake gear on one side only, a second set being added in later years. Note the letters 'SECR', just visible on the upper bodyside panels. *D. J. Wigley*

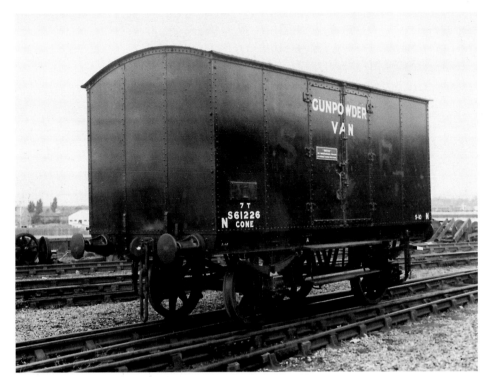

Left:

Plate 192 Ten steel-underframed vans were completed by the Metropolitan Railway Carriage & Wagon Co in 1900, SECR numbers being 3311-20, later SR Nos 61236-45, whilst a further batch of seven was built at Ashford in 1913. These were SECR Nos 1664-70, replacing some SER vehicles which had carried the same numbers. The later Southern numbers were 61223-9. All were included on SR diagram 1703, despite some minor variations in dimensions. No S61226 was photographed at Ashford Works in 1949, freshly painted in SR brown livery with the company letters replaced by the 'S' prefix to the number. The former SR and SECR company initials are still visible beneath the new paint finish. Only three of the 23 vans failed to make British Railways stock and the rest remained in service until the 1955-60 period. *National Railway Museum*

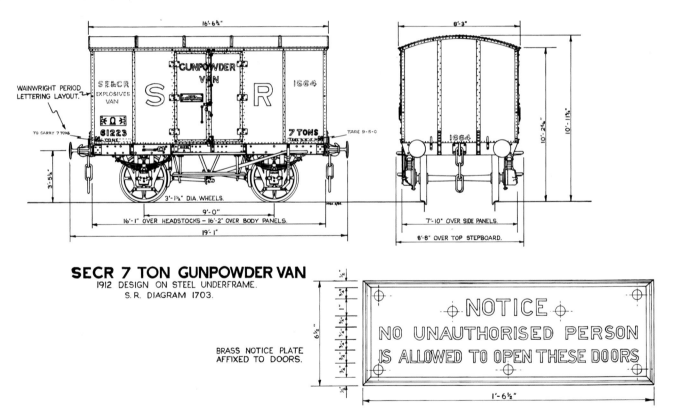

SECR 7 TON GUNPOWDER VAN
1912 DESIGN ON STEEL UNDERFRAME.
S. R. DIAGRAM 1703.

Above:
Figure 72 This figure depicts the 1912 design, although the 1900 steel-underframed vehicles differ only in detail. It also shows the restricted access notice which appears on all these vans. Presumably the temporary gunpowder vans also had similar notices affixed to their doors. It is not known what other modifications were made to these vans. The lettering style shown above for the SECR period is based on an undated Ashford drawing and has not been confirmed by photographic evidence. Some gunpowder traffic was carried in private-owner vans, as portrayed in **Plate 146** on page 108.

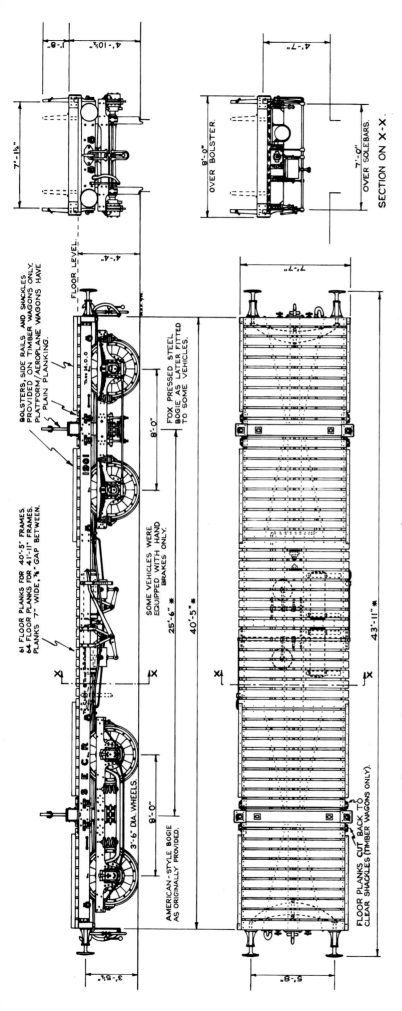

SECR 6 TON BOGIE PLATFORM/TIMBER WAGON (EX-CARRIAGE STOCK UNDERFRAMES IN 1917/18)

S.R. DIAGRAMS 1101 (40'-5" LONG) & 1102 (41'-11" LONG). THE S.R. CLASSIFICATION WAS FLAT AEROPLANE TRUCK.
DIMENSIONS MARKED * REFER TO DIAGRAM 1101. FOR DIAGRAM 1102 ADD 1'-6".

Above:
Figure 73 This figure shows the 1917-18 aeroplane trucks. Towards the end of World War 1 most railways found it necessary to provide some vehicles for the conveyance of aeroplane parts. The SECR utilised several former carriage underframes dating from 1878/9 for this purpose. They were stripped of bodywork and had transverse planking substituted. They also retained their old carriage stock numbers, which fell between 1892 and 1937, being converted in 1917/18. Some were sent overseas via Richborough train ferry, some went to the LNWR, but the SECR retained at least 30 examples. Four had bolsters added in 1921 and these were then allocated to the engineer's department at Angerstein Wharf for use as timber or rail carriers. Two of these received Southern Railway departmental stock numbers 0729S and 0730S, lasting until 1928. The rest were all withdrawn between 1921 and 1924 and none of the 10 survivors at the Grouping received their allocated SR passenger van stock series numbers, which would have been 4197-206. Details of these 10 wagons, plus the engineer's vehicles are as follows:
SR diagram 1101 — SECR Nos 1900/3/4/5/7-10 (Nos 1894, 1901/2 as ED stock).
SR diagram 1102 — SECR Nos 1918/19 (No 1914 as ED stock).

Right:
Plate 193 One of the longer examples of the 1917/18 aeroplane trucks, either SECR No 1921/2/3 or 1928, at Canterbury West in August 1921, loaded with a former North London Railway coach body. This carries both a War Department number and the words 'Lot 5040' painted on the end, so may have been sold off from Richborough Port as part of the postwar rundown of that establishment. *H. P. Rutherford*

137

Chapter 10.
Engineer's Department Wagons

Included in this section are those wagons used by the engineer's department to maintain the permanent way and structures. We will deal with those wagons which were renumbered into the Southern Railway's main numbering sequence, ie ballast wagons, ballast brake vans and rail wagons. The engineer's department also owned a considerable amount of other stock such as cranes, stores vans, yard wagons and the like, but these are outside the scope of our survey. Most of these were numbered in the departmental stock list; this was certainly so after 1923 but in SECR days some were to be found in the general wagon numbering series.

Engineer's department wagons could be met with at any location, but the main depots prior to 1923 were at Angerstein Wharf (SER) and Faversham Creek (LCDR). The Southern Railway set up new depots at Hither Green and Ashford in the 1940s. Shingle for ballasting and drainage work was obtained from the Dungeness branch, but better quality ballast in the form of Kentish ragstone came from near Sevenoaks and, commencing in 1903, from Allington Quarry, south of Aylesford. This latter source continued to provide material for track ballasting until the 1950s.

Twelve Southern Railway diagrams concern us here and these are listed below together with several SECR diagrams, the vehicles of which were extant at the Grouping but for which no SR diagram was allocated, probably because they had a short life expectancy.

SR Diagram	SECR Diagram	Origin	Capacity (tons)	Vehicle Type	Length Over Headstocks	Wheel-base	Known Period of Construction	Remarks
1326	s1061	LCDR	6 and 8	Three-plank dropside	15ft 0in	9ft 3in	1876-99	See Chapter 3.
1741	s1071	SER	6 and 8	Two-plank dropside	12ft 6in	7ft 6in	1874-1900	Dumb-buffers.
1742	s1071/1	SER	6, 7 and 8	Two-plank dropside	12ft 6in	7ft 6in	Rebuilt c1913 onwards	Sprung buffers.
–	s1037 and s1037/1	SER	6, 7, 8 and 10	Three-plank dropside	15ft 0in	8ft 6in	Psd 1897-1901 from Wm Jones	Some with . dumb-buffers
1743	s1055	SECR	8 and 10	Three-plank dropside	14ft 11in	9ft 0in	1904-16	Replacements for above.
1744	s2139/4	SECR	12, some later 10	Two-plank dropside	17ft 0in	9ft 6in	1919-23	Maunsell/Lynes design.
1745	s1048	SECR	20	Ballast hopper	19ft 0in	12ft 0in	1911}	Built by Leeds Forge
1746	s1048	SECR	20	Ballast hopper	21ft 0in	12ft 6in	1915}	Co.
–	Unknown	LCDR	8 and 10	Ballast brake van	18ft 0in	9ft 6in	Prob 1880s	Only four known.
1747	s1066	SER	10	Ballast brake van	19ft 6in	10ft 3in	1865 and 1899-1912	Several designs.
1748	s3489	SECR	20	Ballast plough and brake van	25ft 0in	18ft 0in	1914	Three more built 1932.
–	s1054	SECR	12	Open goods (rail trucks)	15ft 5in	9ft 4in	1904	Numbered as open wagons.
1794	s1351	SECR	30	Bogie rail wagon	45ft 0in	Bogies ccs 34ft 0in	1906/7	Built by C. Roberts.
1795	s2139/9	SECR	35	Bogie rail wagon	50ft 0in	Bogie ccs 40ft 6in	1920	One later to diagram 1796.
1796	–	SECR	35	Bogie rail wagon	54ft 0in	Bogie ccs 40ft 6in	Rebuilt 2/37	Ex-diagram 1795.

The LCDR ballast wagons were identical to their traffic department dropside open goods wagons to SR diagram 1326, but were numbered 6001-40 in LCDR ownership to distinguish them from the traffic department wagons. The only known photograph shows them to be lettered somewhat differently from the traffic department dropside wagons. The letters 'LCDR' appear to be absent, but in the centre of the lower plank of each side are two lines of lettering — perhaps 'Engineer's Department', or something similar. Some or perhaps all these vehicles were traffic department cast-offs. These are drawn and described on pages 20 and 21. In addition to those wagons listed above, the SECR purchased 100 four-plank dropside wagons from the contractors Price and Reeves in 1901/2. Although eminently suitable for engineering work, they were classed as open goods wagons by the SECR and later became SR diagram 1352. These are drawn and described on page 46.

The South Eastern companies did not choose to adopt a different livery for their engineer's department stock, the standard light red or various shades of grey being employed. After 1923 the Southern Railway adopted red oxide for its engineer's vehicles in marked contrast with the dark brown on most other goods vehicles. Ballast brake vans would have received the usual Venetian red ends in SR days, but it is not certain if ex-SER ballast brake vans followed the goods brake van livery in the years before 1899.

Left:

Left:

Plate 194 Typical of the two-plank dumb-buffered dropside ballast wagons is SER No 4313 at Folkestone Harbour in 1882, in a rake of at least six similar vehicles. The letter 'B' presumably indicates a ballast wagon, but by 1899 the vehicles were usually lettered 'Engineer's Dept' along the top plank. Construction of these vehicles spanned a long period, so it is not certain if all were the same. From circa 1912 a start was made on replacing the dumb-buffers with self-contained sprung ones, but at least half of those remaining in use in 1923 were still in original condition. *L&GRP*

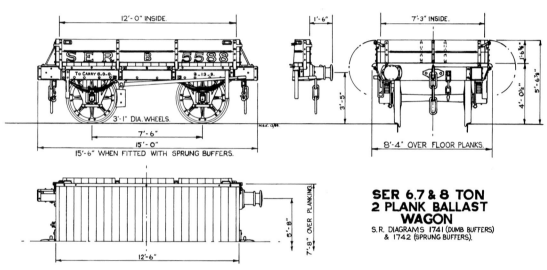

SER 6,7 & 8 TON 2 PLANK BALLAST WAGON
S.R. DIAGRAMS 1741 (DUMB BUFFERS) & 1742 (SPRUNG BUFFERS).

Above:
Figure 74 A combined drawing of the two-plank ballast wagons to diagrams 1741 and 1742. Examples of SER numbers are as follows. Diagram 1741: Nos 1611/26/38, 3178-97, 4243/64. 4331/6/54/61, 4682, 4753, 7226. Diagram 1742: Nos 1631/3/4/44, 2406, 4233/45/75/6, 4301/28, 4581, 4974, 7234, 7451/4. The final survivors were withdrawn circa 1930. Dumb-buffered wagons were banned from main line service after 1915 but could be used as ballast wagons until at least the mid-1920s. SR numbers may be found in Appendix 1 on page 159.

Left:
Plate 195 Between 1897 and 1901 the South Eastern purchased 200 wagons from William Jones, a contractor who also dealt in secondhand rolling stock, allocating to them numbers 2559-68, 2615-80, 2991-3040, 3100-49, plus random numbers between 4235 and 4305. No 2564, one of those purchased in 1897, was photographed about 1901, still carrying SER livery. Note the canvas flaps over the axleboxes and double-block brake gear on one side only. SECR diagram s1037 was allocated. *L&GRP*

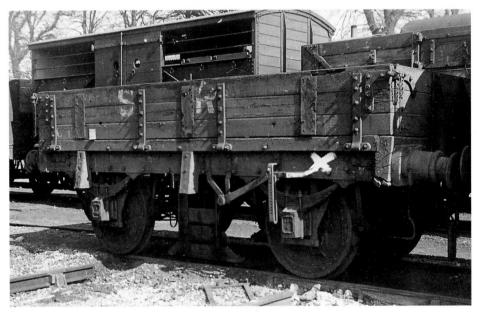

Left:

Plate 196 From about 1912 many of the former Wm Jones wagons were reconstructed with self-contained sprung buffers, to SECR diagram s1037/1. In this form at least some of the 39 survivors at the Grouping were allocated numbers in the range 62093, 62139-75 and 62366. Few were actually renumbered but at least three entered SR departmental stock. No 226S was formerly SECR No 4298 and was at first allocated SR ballast wagon No 62175. It later became Feltham Yard brush wagon 226S in late 1925, and was photographed there in May 1934. The brush gear was used to keep the rails clean so that the dc current track circuits installed there worked satisfactorily. The wagon had been reconstructed in March 1913 and was withdrawn in July 1936. *R. W. Kidner*

Centre left:

Plate 197 A similar brush wagon to that shown in the previous plate, No 631S is seen at Ashford about 1948. This was lettered 'Rail Cleaning Wagon' on the solebar and was based at Earlswood, on the Brighton Section. Formerly SECR No 2638, it became SR ballast wagon No 62143 after the Grouping and entered departmental service in 1932. Reconstructed in 1913, it was almost certainly the final survivor of the Wm Jones wagons. *E. B. Trotter*

Below left:

Plate 198 Replacements for the various dumb-buffered wagons were built from 1904 onwards. SR diagram 1743 was allocated and 190 such vehicles were completed, but not in numerical order. SECR numbers were random between 1627 and 4376, replacing vehicles to diagrams 1741, 1742 and Wm Jones wagons, but two replaced LCDR Nos 11828/42. At least six are visible in this 1925 view of a bank slip at Smeeth. *Southern Railway Magazine*

Right:

Plate 199 The Maunsell/Lynes contribution was a two-plank vehicle, the prototype of which is illustrated opposite. Built on the standardised steel underframe, No 11835 was outshopped in March 1919, the first of 120 examples completed over the next four years. It is doubtful if many production examples were lettered as shown — most being as drawn in **Figure 76** on page 142. It is believed that all 120 entered traffic in SECR livery, although some were not completed until mid-1923. The extended floor planking was later cut back flush with the dropsides. No 11835 subsequently became SR No 62407 and ran until the 1960s. *SECR Official*

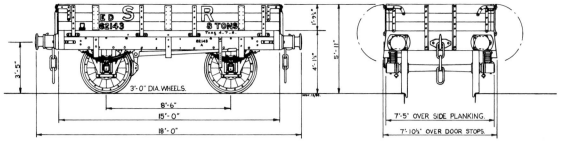

SER 6,8 & 10 TON 3 PLANK BALLAST WAGON AS RECONSTRUCTED CIRCA 1912/13.
SOME LATER ALLOCATED TO S.R. DIAGRAM 1743.

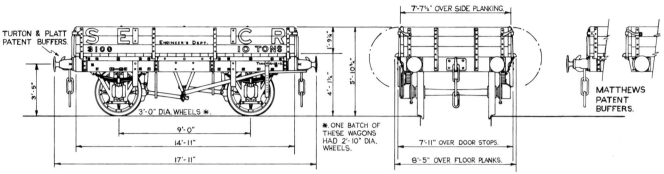

SECR 8 & 10 TON 3 PLANK BALLAST WAGON WITH SECONDHAND LCDR WHEELSETS.
S.R. DIAGRAM 1743.

Above:
Figure 75 This figure illustrates both types of SER/SECR three-plank dropside ballast wagon. Some of the reconstructed examples were also allocated to SR diagram 1743, although the dimensions varied somewhat from those built new between 1904 and 1916. The last survivor was SR No 62356 (ex-SECR No 4272), which ran from March 1916 until October 1952. Examples of numbering are as follows:

Ex-William Jones vehicles
SECR Nos 3025, 2615/20, 2991, 3001/33, 3113/43, 4262, 3127; these became SR Nos 62093, 62139/41/50/3/9/65/71/4 and 62366 respectively.

Diagram 1743 vehicles

SECR Nos	Survivors to SR Nos	Date Built	Brake Gear	Buffers
2688-97	62258-65	1905	DB	Turton & Platt's Patent
2569-73	62200-3	1905	DB	Turton & Platt's Patent
3100/6	62303/8	1906	DB	Turton & Platt's Patent
2618, 3011	62205/85	1909	DB	Matthews Patent
2564-8	62195-9	1913	F	Matthews Patent
2986-90	62269-73	1913	F	Matthews Patent

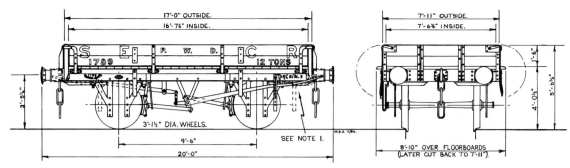

SECR 12 TON 2 PLANK BALLAST WAGON
S.R. DIAGRAM 1744.

NOTE I. ALTERNATIVE POSITION OF BRAKE RACK AND SHAPE OF BRAKE
LEVER SHOWN BY BROKEN LINES.

Above:
Figure 76 SECR 12-ton two-plank wagon, SR diagram 1744.

Left:
Plate 200 Diagram 1744 wagon No S62372 at Yeovil Pen Mill in September 1961. This was formerly SECR No 1759. Examples of SECR numbering are 477-81, 546-51, 1754-93 and 11873-82. The livery is unpainted timber with reddish-brown panels and black numbering patches. Several of these vehicles were allocated to Broad Clyst depot and were lost to the Western Region in January 1963. Note the different shape of the brake lever, compared to SECR No 11835. *A. E. West*

Right:
Plate 201 A feature of some of these wagons in the 1950s was their almost complete absence of lettering. This anonymous example, possibly SR No 62444, carries nothing more than a 'Return to Ashford Kent' instruction on its red oxide paint finish. Notice that it is coupled in a rake of similar vehicles. The photograph was taken at Ashford in July 1950. Some of these wagons received the BR ballast wagon code name of 'Sole'. *A. E. West*

Right:
Plate 202 Another example, No S62388 (ex-SECR No 1775), is seen at Eastleigh in August 1962. This carries well-worn black livery with yellow lettering. Also visible is the SECR either-side or lift-link brake gear. Several of these wagons lasted until 1971, by which time they were among the last pre-Grouping wagons in the Southern Region CCE fleet, excluding the Isle of Wight, where some Price & Reeves ballast wagons and a few ex-LSWR and LBSCR vehicles were still in use. *A. E. West*

Plate 203 A number of brake vans were specially constructed for ballast train use and the SER contribution was remarkably long-lived. SR No 62518 is seen at Hoo Junction in September 1931 and was already 56 years old when photographed. It would last until April 1936. Eight such vans were built as long ago as 1865, SER numbers being 3929-36. All except No 3933 became SR stock as Nos 62513-19, diagram number 1747 being allocated. Van No 3933 was in fact replaced by a new vehicle in 1912 but was very similar in appearance to the original. This became SR No 62512. *R. W. Kidner*

Following the Wainwright tradition, an additional 12 almost identical vans were ordered from Metropolitan Railway Carriage & Wagon Co in 1899/1900, SECR numbers being 3088-99. Again, one failed to become SR stock but the rest were renumbered as SR 62501-11. The bodywork was almost identical to the SER vehicles, but instead of the grease-lubricated axleboxes and slide brakes (just visible on No 62518) the new vans employed oil axleboxes and eight brake blocks and are the subject of **Figure 77** on the next page. The last survivor of the Metropolitan batch was SR No 62505, destroyed by enemy action in April 1941.

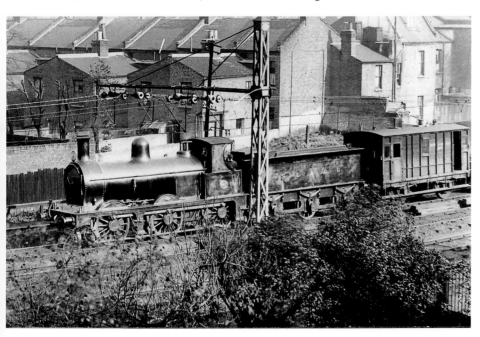

Left:
Plate 204 Four more vans were completed by the company between 1899 and 1912. The 1912 van (SECR No 3933) has already been mentioned, but the other three were replacements for LCDR ballast brakes and took SECR numbers 11868/71/2, later becoming SR Nos 62520-2. These, however, appear to be different to the rest, although this fact is not recorded on either the SECR or SR diagrams. One of these vans is seen at Shepherds Lane, Brixton, about 1912/13. It appears to be SECR No 11872, but this is not entirely certain. If correctly identified, the van dates from 1911 and ran until late 1949, being the last survivor of the type. Also visible is LCDR 'B' class 0-6-0 No 597. Note the LBSCR overhead electrification equipment on the adjacent South London line. *S. A. W. Harvey*

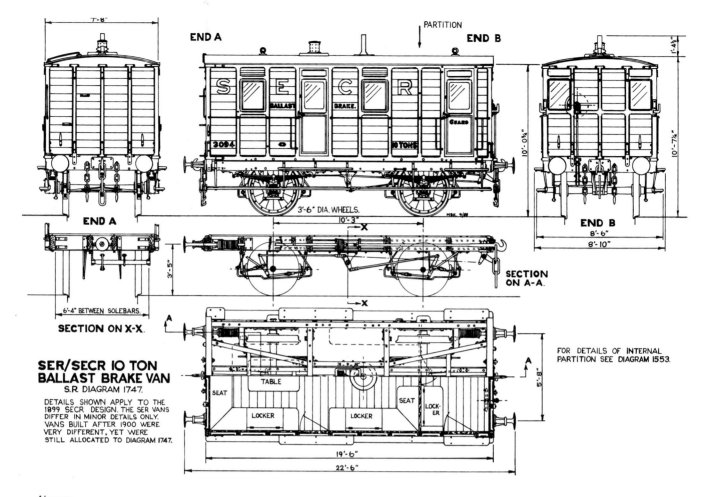

END A   PARTITION   END B

7'-8"

S E C R

BALLAST.   BRAKE.   GEARS

3094   10 TONS

3'-6" DIA. WHEELS.

10'-0¾"

1'-4½"

10'-7¼"

END A   10'-3"   X

3'-5"

SECTION ON A-A.

END B

8'-6"

8'-10"

6'-4" BETWEEN SOLEBARS.

SECTION ON X-X.

SER/SECR 10 TON BALLAST BRAKE VAN
S.R. DIAGRAM 1747.

DETAILS SHOWN APPLY TO THE 1899 SECR DESIGN. THE SER VANS DIFFER IN MINOR DETAILS ONLY. VANS BUILT AFTER 1900 WERE VERY DIFFERENT, YET WERE STILL ALLOCATED TO DIAGRAM 1747.

SEAT   TABLE   LOCKER   LOCKER   SEAT   LOCKER

5'-8"

19'-6"

22'-6"

FOR DETAILS OF INTERNAL PARTITION SEE DIAGRAM 1553.

Above:

Figure 77 This figure shows what may be termed the 'standard' version of SER/SECR ballast brake van, as built in 1865, 1899/1900 and 1912. One of the three LCDR replacement vans was actually built at Longhedge in 1899, so it might be of LCDR origin, but the actual bodywork design is not known for certain. The cost of these vehicles makes an interesting comparison: those built in 1865 are recorded as costing a mere £98 each, those by Metropolitan in 1900 were £200 apiece, whilst the four odd vans varied between £142 and £173 each. All were equipped to provide both guard's and riding accommodation for the permanent way gangs, in two separate compartments.

Right:

Plate 205 Another odd van, perhaps SECR No 11868 or 11871, is seen at the head of a down ballast train approaching Ashford in September 1924 behind 'O1' class 0-6-0 No 426. As will be seen, this van is similar but not identical to the 'standard' version. It also has modern axleboxes. No 11868 was completed at Longhedge in 1899 whilst No 11871 was built at Ashford in 1903. They ran until the late 1930s. A note in the SECR register states that no new drawing was prepared for these additional vans, and also that no diagram number was allocated for No 11868. The authors are therefore unable to identify these three vans further. Perhaps the details were worked out by the wagon shop staff rather than in the drawing office. Also visible in the photograph are some ballast wagons to diagrams 1743 and 1744, plus the extensive cattle and sheep handling facilities at Ashford market. *F. J. Agar*

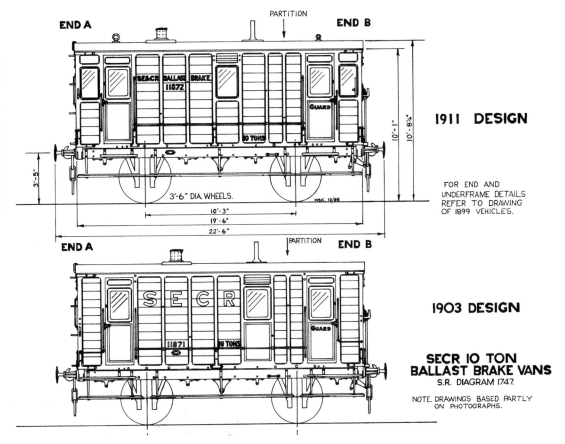

Right:

Figure 78 A drawing of the two ballast brake vans seen in **Plates 204** and **205**. Although numbered as 11871 and 11872, it is possible that one of the vehicles is that built at Longhedge in 1899 (SECR No 11868). The drawing is based on photographs and the 'standard' diagram 1747 design, so is not guaranteed to be completely accurate.

1911 DESIGN

FOR END AND UNDERFRAME DETAILS REFER TO DRAWING OF 1899 VEHICLES.

1903 DESIGN

SECR 10 TON BALLAST BRAKE VANS
S.R. DIAGRAM 1747.

NOTE. DRAWINGS BASED PARTLY ON PHOTOGRAPHS.

Right:

Plate 206 Very little is known about earlier LCDR ballast brake vans. Only four have so far been traced: LCDR Nos 203/5/6/7, later SECR Nos 11868/70-2. Three were replaced by the diagram 1747 vans built in 1899, 1903 and 1911, whilst No 11870 was converted into a stores van in 1911 for the engineer's department. None became SR stock at the Grouping but in order to complete our history of Chatham Section vehicles this photograph and **Figure 79** have been included. This is the only known photograph and was taken at Faversham about 1904.
Dr Evers, courtesy R. L. Ratcliffe

Below:

Figure 79 This figure is also based partly on the accompanying photograph and partly on the drawing for the standard LCDR goods brake van as illustrated on page 105 so is also not guaranteed to be completely accurate.

LC & DR BALLAST BRAKE VAN

NO SR DIAGRAM - DRAWING BASED ON PHOTOGRAPHS ONLY.

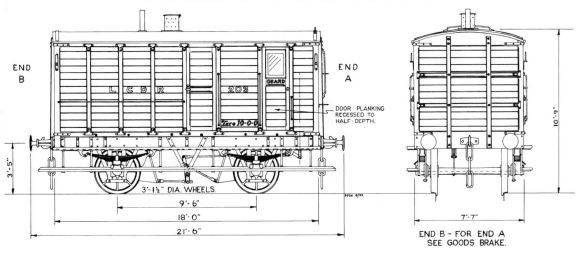

Right:

Plate 207 The old order in SECR ballast trains, near Shoreham (Kent) in 1926. 'O' class 0-6-0 No A52 heads a train consisting of a diagram 1747 ballast brake followed by 20 ballast wagons, mostly to diagram 1743 but three vehicles to diagram 1744 are visible. Some remain in pre-Grouping livery. What is probably another diagram 1747 brake is at the rear. *Dr I. C. Allen*

Left:

Plate 208 The new order in SECR ballast trains is seen at Orpington in August 1923. 'O' class 0-6-0 No 376 hauls a train consisting of the inevitable diagram 1747 ballast brake, six of the 1911 ballast hoppers to diagram 1745 and one 1915 example to diagram 1746, identifiable by its side door. The last vehicle is the (then) unique ballast plough and brake van to diagram 1748, SECR No 6330. Note that it has been relettered in the Maunsell-period style. *K. Nunn/LCGB Collection*

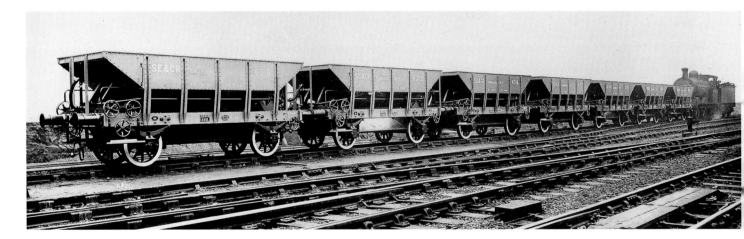

Above:

Plate 209 In former years track ballasting or reballasting was an extremely labour-intensive process. The introduction of the ballast hopper wagon on several railways around the turn of the 20th century was an important step forward, although the early designs all suffered from two defects. They discharged their loads only down the centre of the track, and once the door had been opened it could not be closed until the wagon was completely empty. The spreading of the ballast was achieved by the use of a ballast plough, but the rate of discharge and effectiveness of the spreading process remained a matter of fine judgement. The SECR ordered seven hoppers from The Leeds Forge Co in 1911 and these are seen about to leave the company's premises. Compare the lettering style with that shown in the official view, reproduced opposite. The production finish included black buffers and running gear, the lettering 'Engineer's Dept.' being added on each side. The wagon number was placed on the left-hand end of the hopper instead of in the centre. *Leeds Forge Co*

Above:

Plate 210 In 1910 the Leeds Forge Co came up with the answer to both the ballasting and reballasting problems with a patent design that provided controllable rotating doors, giving discharge to either side, or the middle, or any combination that might be needed. The first wagons built under the patent were for the Buenos Aires Western Railway in 1911, but in the following year the SECR took delivery of the first seven for use in Britain. These were of 20 tons capacity and were constructed from pressed steel plates in the usual Leeds Forge manner. SECR numbers were 6316-22 and their cost is recorded at £260 each. In comparison, a 12-ton mineral wagon then cost about £80. No 6316 is finished in two-tone photographic grey livery, with a slightly different lettering style to that eventually specified. The three hand wheels at the right-hand end operate the doors; that at the left-hand end operates the hand brake. Vacuum brakes were also provided, the release cord being visible at the left-hand end. All seven were officially uprated to 21 tons in 1938 but it was February 1950 before No 6316 was so painted, probably when it acquired the BR livery of black with yellow lettering. As DS62487, it ran until October 1955. *Leeds Forge Co*

147

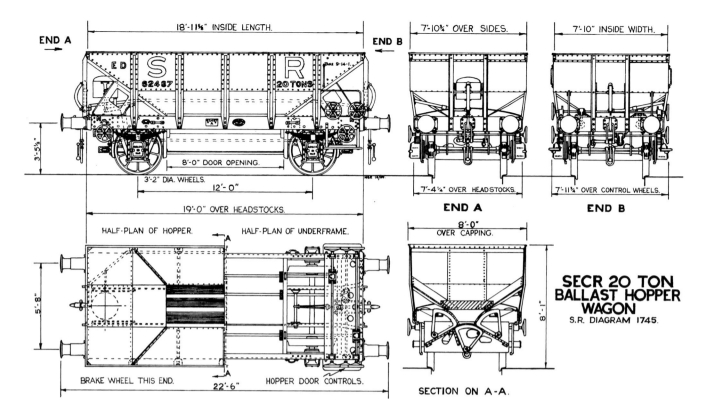

END A

18'-11¾" INSIDE LENGTH.

END B

7'-10½" OVER SIDES.

7'-10" INSIDE WIDTH.

E D

S R
62487

20 TONS

3'-5½"

8'-0" DOOR OPENING.

3'-2" DIA. WHEELS.

12'-0"

19'-0" OVER HEADSTOCKS.

7'-4½" OVER HEADSTOCKS.

7'-11¾" OVER CONTROL WHEELS.

END A

END B

HALF-PLAN OF HOPPER.

HALF-PLAN OF UNDERFRAME.

8'-0"
OVER CAPPING.

5'-8"

8'-1"

BRAKE WHEEL THIS END.

22'-6"

HOPPER DOOR CONTROLS.

SECTION ON A-A.

SECR 20 TON
BALLAST HOPPER
WAGON
S.R. DIAGRAM 1745.

Above:
Figure 80 A drawing of the 1911 hopper, to SR diagram 1745. SR numbers were 62487-93 and all ran until the 1950s, seemingly without modification. Following several months in service, the *Railway Gazette* published an article on the vehicles in which it was claimed that, under recent trials, one of these hoppers loaded with Kentish ragstone, broken to a suitable gauge, discharged its contents over a distance of 50yd in less than two minutes. The ballast was then spread by two men at the rate of 4ft of track per minute. This was a considerable improvement over the traditional methods of using dropside ballast wagons and produced a great saving in manpower.

In service the 1911 wagons were very successful, but running alongside a moving train and operating the control wheels was a dangerous business. Accordingly in 1915, the Leeds Forge Co delivered a second train of seven hoppers where the control wheels for the discharge mechanisms were mounted on the end of the wagon. The operator now travelled on the vehicle and this marked a very considerable advance in the design of British ballast hoppers. To accommodate the controls, the hopper was foreshortened by 18in at one end only and this, together with the uneven overhang, gave a somewhat unusual appearance. **Plate 211** *(below)* illustrates one of these wagons, SR No 62495, in post-1936 livery at Ashford in 1946. Delivered in December 1915 as SECR No 6324, at a cost of £323, it was uprated to 21 tons capacity in December 1938 and lasted until February 1960. *E. B. Trotter*

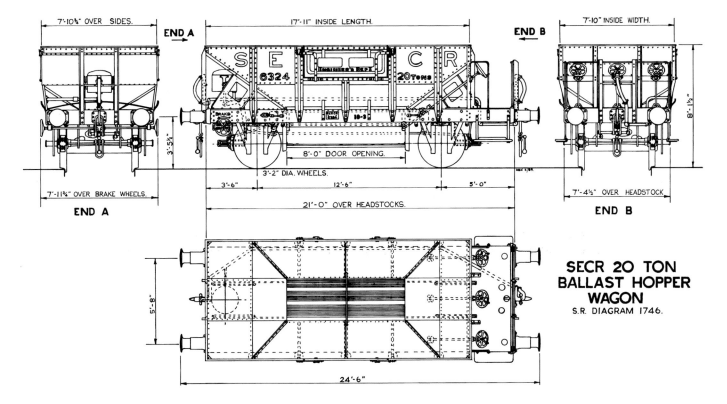

The diagram shows dimensions including:
7'-10¾" OVER SIDES.
END A →
17'-11" INSIDE LENGTH.
← END B
7'-10" INSIDE WIDTH.
S E C R
6324 20 TONS
3'-5⅛"
7'-11¾" OVER BRAKE WHEELS.
END A
8'-0" DOOR OPENING.
3'-2" DIA. WHEELS.
3'-6" 12'-6" 5'-0"
21'-0" OVER HEADSTOCKS.
7'-4½" OVER HEADSTOCK.
8'-1½"
END B
5'-8"
24'-6"

SECR 20 TON BALLAST HOPPER WAGON
S.R. DIAGRAM 1746.

Above:
Figure 81 The 1915 design of ballast hopper to SR diagram 1746, showing the SECR style of lettering. The unusual asymmetrical arrangement subsequently became commonplace as both the LNER and, to a limited extent, the LMS used the design, although it was not until British Railway days that it became widespread over the whole country. The BR 'Herring', 'Trout' and 'Dogfish' are all developed from the 1915 Leeds Forge design.

Right:
Plate 212 Diagram 1746 hopper SR No 62498 at Meldon, Devon, in July 1948, together with 1911 vehicle No 62492. This shows the opposite end of the wagon, with vacuum cylinder instead of the discharge mechanism. SECR Nos for these vehicles were 6323-9, later SR Nos 62494-500. All lasted into the 1960s. Also visible is an ex-LSWR hopper to diagram 1734 and a Southern Railway bogie 40-ton vehicle. The ramshackle locomotive shed was temporary home to LSWR 'O2' 0-4-4T No 232, deputising for the regular engine — LCDR 'T' class 0-6-0 No 500S. *J. H. Aston*

As the above picture shows, these SECR hoppers worked to Meldon Quarry in Southern days, but they never lost their connections with Allington Quarry and several of them could still be seen there in the 1950s.

The next logical step was the provision of vehicles capable of spreading the ballast using ploughs. Although the *Railway Gazette* article praised the speed at which two men spread the ballast once it had been discharged from the hopper, few permanent way staff could keep up such a rate for very long.

The SECR built just one such ballast plough — a 20-ton long-wheelbased vehicle completed at Ashford in June 1914. This was equipped with two retractable ploughs mounted within the wheelbase, capable of being raised and lowered using control wheels and locking mechanisms inside the vehicle. Although perfectly acceptable as a plough, the brake was unpopular with the guards and permanent way men alike, due to the amount of machinery within the van. The risk of injury through being thrown against all this gear was only too real.

Above:

Plate 213 The 20-ton ballast plough brake van No 6330 is seen when new in June 1914. The drawings for this van were prepared in 1910, no doubt in conjunction with the first train of hoppers. However, it was thought that a plough van might not be necessary, so construction was postponed for some years. With hindsight, it was considered useful, so when the second train of hoppers was ordered the idea was revived. No 6330 was not cheap, costing almost £545, but it proved effective and in 1932 the Southern ordered three more very similar vans, to be followed in 1949 by a further eight. These vans were normally used only with the hopper trains, even if the ploughs themselves were not always used. Indeed, they could not be when passing over pointwork or near conductor rails. Some staff considered them best left alone! Despite misgivings, this van had a long and hard life. When the Southern Region adopted air brakes in the 1980s these vans migrated far and wide. No 6330, by then numbered DS62523, was noted at locations as far afield as St Blazey and Nottingham. It ran until 1989, by which time it was the last SECR vehicle in use on British Railways. Today it is preserved by the Midland Railway Trust at Butterley. It has lost its original numberplates, but happily one of these is privately preserved in Kent. *SECR Official*

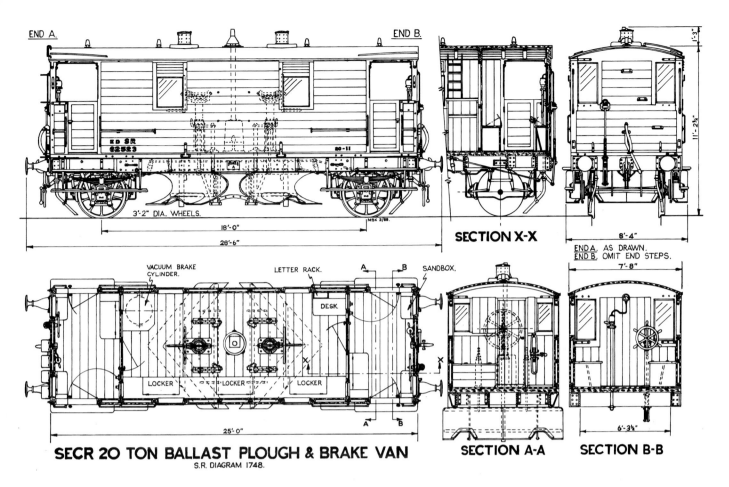

SECR 2O TON BALLAST PLOUGH & BRAKE VAN
S.R. DIAGRAM 1748.

END A.   **END B.**

ED SR
62523

3'-2" DIA. WHEELS.

18'-0"

28'-6"

SECTION X-X

8'-4"

ENDA. AS DRAWN.
ENDB. OMIT END STEPS.

7'-8"

VACUUM BRAKE CYLINDER.

LETTER RACK.

DESK.

SANDBOX.

LOCKER   LOCKER   LOCKER

25'-0"

6'-3½"

SECTION A-A   **SECTION B-B**

Above:

Figure 82 The diagram 1748 ballast plough and brake van. The 1949 vans differ in detail and will be described in Volume 4.

Left:

Plate 214 One of the 1932 SR vans, No 62030, seen at Tonbridge in August 1932. Note the non-standard SR lettering, exactly as specified on the contract drawings. These three vans were built by Charles Roberts & Co and carried ED red oxide with Venetian red ends. Torpedo roof vents and standard SR-type self-contained buffers are fitted. The SR numbers of the three were 62030-2. *H. F. Wheeller*

Below left:

Plate 215 SECR No 6330, as running at Eastleigh in September 1959, now numbered DS62523. Apart from removal of oil lamps and roof vents, the only other obvious alterations are the replacement of the nearest buffer with one of SR pattern, provision of disc wheels and the addition of a Southern standard label clip. Despite all the changes, the tare weight has reduced by just 1cwt. Livery is black with yellow lettering. *A. E. West*

Above:
Plate 216 In 1906 the company ordered 12 30-ton bogie rail wagons from Charles Roberts & Co of Horbury Junction, near Wakefield. Numbered 6077-88, they were delivered from November 1906 to February 1907 and cost £369 apiece. SR numbers were 64604-15 and all ran until the late 1950s. No 6082 (SR 64609) was recorded by the makers, although the lettering layout seems to have been amended before the vehicles entered traffic. *C. Roberts & Co*

Left:
Plate 217 Track blanketing work is in progress in 1947, in Clapham Cutting. Diagram 1794 rail wagon No 64611 is in attendance. The bolster stanchions have been demounted to assist in the unloading of prefabricated track panels. The stanchions may be seen in the bed of the wagon, attached to it by chains. The appearance of the permanent way gang and their supervisors is very typical of the period, without a high-visibility vest or hard hat in sight. *SR Official*

Below left:
Plate 218 The Fox pressed steel bogie under No 64608 at Ashford in July 1950. These bogies were probably more common overseas than in Britain.
A. E. West

Opposite:
Plate 219 Wagon No 6077, photographed outside Ashford Works before entering service. Compare the lettering with that of No 6082 above.
SECR Official

Opposite:
Figure 83 A drawing of the 30-ton bogie rail wagon to SR diagram 1794.

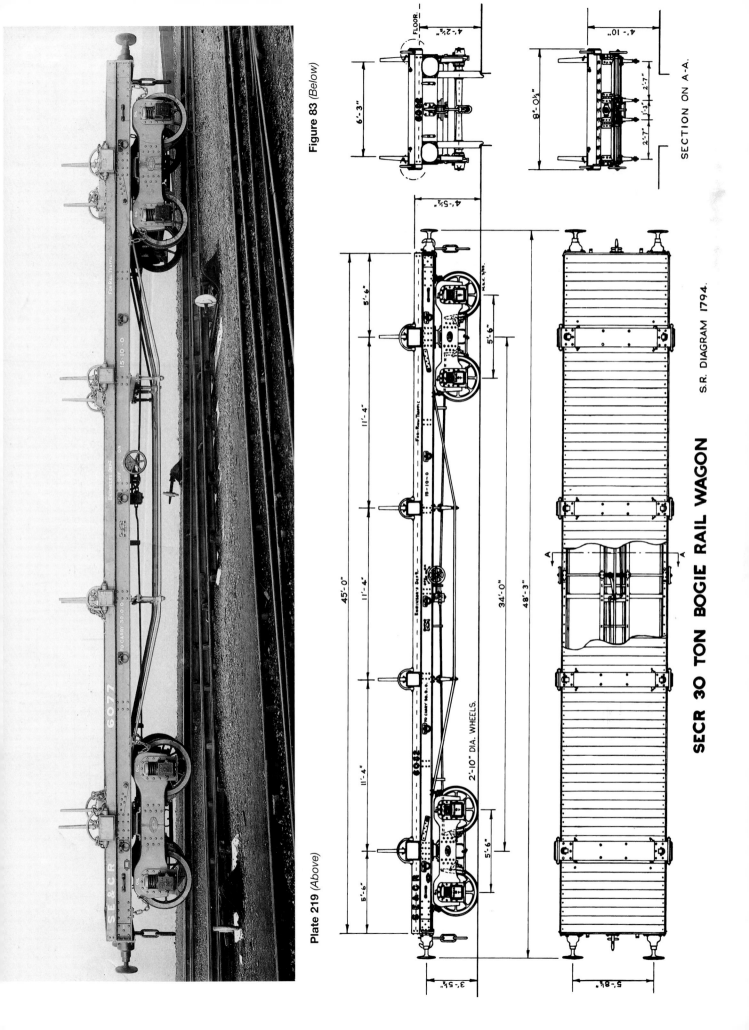

Plate 219 (Above)

Figure 83 (Below)

SECTION ON A-A.

S.R. DIAGRAM 1794.

SECR 30 TON BOGIE RAIL WAGON

Above:
Plate 220 Six more bogie rail wagons were completed at Ashford Works in late 1920, SECR numbers being 6089-94, later SR Nos 64616-21. Designed under Maunsell/Lynes, they were almost a carbon-copy of the then current GWR designs, although none on that railway was actually 50ft long. The base colour appears very dark, possibly matching GWR grey livery as now used by the Great Western Society at Didcot. The letters 'P.W.D.' (permanent way department) were in favour in the post-World War 1 period at Ashford. *SECR Official*

Left and right:
Plate 221 and Figure 84 These vehicles were well constructed and all lasted until the late 1960s. No DS64618 was photographed at Three Bridges engineer's yard in January 1962. Note the reversible stanchions — by placing the top pegs into the side rail housings a runway could be formed to allow rails and other loads to be slid off the wagon in safety. **Figure 84** (*opposite*) makes the arrangement clear. *A. Blackburn*

Left:
Plate 222 No DS64621 is seen at Hoo Junction in the early 1970s, by then carrying the BR wagon code 'Borail'. The livery is black with stencilled white lettering. The heavy steel angle trussing is clearly visible in this view. *D. Larkin*

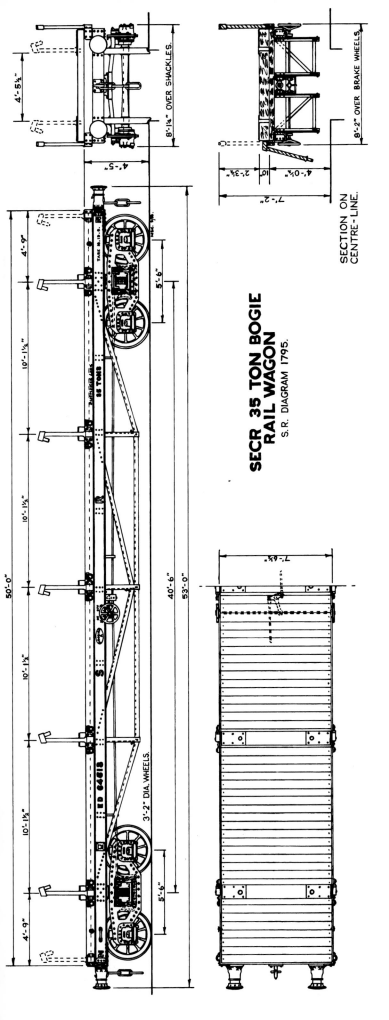

SECR 35 TON BOGIE RAIL WAGON

S.R. DIAGRAM 1795.

SECTION ON CENTRE-LINE.

Above:
Figure 84 The diagram 1795 bogie rail wagon.

Below:
Plate 223 A close-up of the plate frame bogie on DS64617 at Woking in 1968.
P. Tatlow

Nos 64617-19 were adapted for working with 'Robel' cranes for a short period in 1937; however, they were soon returned to ordinary ED service. No 64616 was lengthened to 54ft in February 1937, for carrying concrete footbridge panels, to Diagram 1796.

The four odd four-wheeled wagons to SECR diagram s1054 were classed as open goods wagons, both before and after the Grouping. No special fittings are shown on the diagram and they appear as very ordinary one-plank open wagons. SECR numbers were 1930-2/4, later allocated SR numbers 14891-4. All four were withdrawn between 1924 and 1928 and no photographs or other details are known to the authors. SECR records state that they were rail trucks, but give no further information. A drawing also exists of a 31ft rail wagon, but the drawing is endorsed 'not adopted'. With a wheelbase of 18ft and hinged one-plank drop sides it looks eminently suitable for rail traffic, but it seems that the management at Ashford thought otherwise and the vehicle was not built. Railway history is full of drawings of one sort or another for things that were never built!

155